I0817972

THE STARS OF BASKETBALL

MIAMI
6
BULLS
23
30
LAKERS
24

THE STARS OF BASKETBALL

THE BEST PLAYERS OF ALL TIME

RODOLPHE GAUDIN

GELDING STREET PRESS

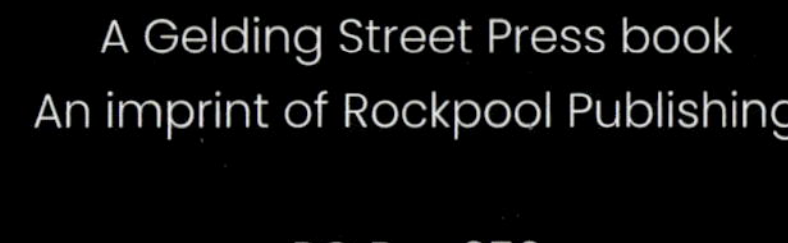

A Gelding Street Press book
An imprint of Rockpool Publishing

PO Box 252
Summer Hill
NSW 2130 Australia

geldingstreetpress.com
Follow us! Geldingstreet_press

This edition published in 2026 by Rockpool Publishing
ISBN: 9781922662408

Design and typesetting by Christine Armstrong, Rockpool Publishing
Translated by Cathlin Barrett
Translation edited by Erin Della Mattia

Printed and bound in China
10 9 8 7 6 5 4 3 2 1

The starting lineup of the Chicago Bulls in 1998. From left to right: Dennis Rodman, Scottie Pippen, Michael Jordan, Ron Harper, and Toni Kukoč.

CONTENTS

Foreword 1

Preface 3

Introduction 5

The backstory 5

Back to basics 5

In the Olympic pantheon 8

The NBA is born! 9

THE LEGENDS

Kareem ABDUL-JABBAR 12

Giannis ANTETOKOUNMPO 16

Carmelo ANTHONY 20

Charles BARKLEY 24

Elgin BAYLOR 28

Larry BIRD 32

Kobe BRYANT 36

Jimmy BUTLER 40

Wilt CHAMBERLAIN 44

Stephen CURRY 48

Luol DENG 52

Luka DONČIĆ 56

Tim DUNCAN 60

Kevin DURANT 64

Joel EMBIID 68

Kevin GARNETT 72

Pau GASOL 76

Rudy GOBERT 80

Allen IVERSON 84

LeBron JAMES 88

Earvin “Magic” JOHNSON 92

Michael JORDAN 96

Toni KUKOČ 100
Luc LONGLEY 104
Karl MALONE 108
Hakeem OLAJUWON 112
Shaquille O'NEAL 116
Tony PARKER 120
Scottie PIPPEN 124
David ROBINSON 128
Dennis RODMAN 132
Bill RUSSELL 136
Predrag STOJAKOVIĆ 140
Isiah THOMAS 144
Klay THOMPSON 148
Russell WESTBROOK 152

LEGENDARY MATCHES

1962: Wilt Chamberlain's unbeatable scoring record 157
1992: The Dream Team on top of Mount Olympus 161
1992: Magic Johnson smiles again 165
1997: The flu game – Michael Jordan, stronger than the flu 169
1998: Michael Jordan's last shot for the Bulls 173
2006: Kobe Bryant scores over 80! 177
2007: Tony Parker raises the French flag at the top of the NBA 181
2013: The coronation of an entire blue generation 185
2021: France, Team USA's new nemesis 189
2024: Stephen Curry takes over Bercy and kills France's dream 193
Photo credits 196

Rudy Gobert during the France-United States group match at the Tokyo Olympics in 2021

FOREWORD

You can't escape your destiny, and mine was to become a basketball player. I tried my hand at other sports – athletics, karate, and even boxing – but sooner or later, the orange ball was bound to catch up with me. And that's what happened at the age of 12. It was in me, and yet I knew nothing about the sport! I didn't watch the games on TV, I didn't have internet access, and my friends wore basketball jerseys of players I didn't know!

I enrolled in a sports-study program at the age of 14. At the Cholet Basket Training Center, I was far from being one of the best of my generation. But I worked hard and developed my skills, with my head full of dreams. At 15, I imagined myself in the NBA and being an All-Star. Lots of people laughed at me! They thought my ambitions were over the top, and I don't blame them. My mother always encouraged me, even though I know it was hard for her to see me leave home. She trusted me and that gave me wings.

I discovered the NBA at the beginning of the LeBron James years. Back then, the star-studded runway was packed – Shaquille O'Neal, the late Kobe Bryant, and so many others. It was enough to leave me awestruck and make me dream of one day being part of that great family. I've never really had a favorite player, but I've spent hours watching videos of LeBron James for the showmanship, and Kevin Garnett, Pau Gasol, and Tim Duncan for their style in my position. They were all sources of inspiration in their own way.

And one day, I found myself face-to-face with them! I couldn't wait to see them in real life and to go head-to-head. I was on the court to win, and that meant destroying them. My main weapon, the one that got me where I am today, is blocking shots. So, I put everything I had into trying to stop my former idols on defense. They'd attack the hoop and I'd be there to block them. The first block of my career on LeBron James? What a thrill! I thought to myself, "I've just blocked the King!" After that, nothing could stop me.

I fulfilled my childhood dreams, but the ultimate goal as a man and an athlete was then to go for an NBA championship title! My transfer from the Utah Jazz to the Minnesota Timberwolves was a step in that direction. I was going to play for a team that could contend for the top spots. Now when I talk about going for the championship ring, it's no longer a laughing matter!

Rudy Gobert

Earvin "Magic" Johnson (32) and Michael Jordan (23) at the 1992 NBA All-Star Game East-West

PREFACE

My favorite number is 23! This number is the stuff of dreams. As a teenager, I'd get up at night to watch it glide across the NBA courts. Embroidered in black on a red background, the number 23 shone brightly and eclipsed all others. Every time he had the ball, a miracle could happen. The talent, the genius, the 23, that's Michael Jordan! More than a basketball player, a brand. The greatest basketball player of all time, the ultimate athlete.

Several years later, in the early 2000s, I began working for the Sunday program ***Stade 2*** on France2, a decision partly inspired by Jordan. The 23 of the Chicago Bulls had become the 23 of the Washington Wizards. Not quite the Jordan of my younger years, but his charisma and aura were still intact. A Jordan interview is really something! That evening, he had crossed paths with a French-American player from the San Antonio Spurs. Tony Parker was just beginning his American career, and the living legend of the orange ball was full of praise for the Spurs' number 9.

Also while working at France Télévisions, I had the privilege of witnessing Tony Parker's first appearance in the starting five in 2001. He exuded an impressive serenity and self-confidence. Three NBA titles later, I ran into Tony again, now a star of the world's biggest basketball league and one of the members of the Spurs' Big Three. It was 2011, on his home turf, and I could almost touch his championship rings. What a long way to come! In the end, he would finish his career with four NBA titles, just two less than "His Airness," His Majesty MJ. I could never have imagined such success for the rookie I used to accompany to the bakery before training to buy doughnuts for his teammates, like Tim Duncan, who became one of his best friends.

Another player admired by Michael Jordan was Kobe Bryant. The late Kobe Bryant was not only his opponent, but also a close friend. A player like no other from the City of Angels. More than just a number, the 8 and then the 24, he was a legend in the most famous NBA franchise. He was always compared (rightly or wrongly) to Jordan. Michael was a true source of inspiration for him, and Kobe dreamed of surpassing him. His change of jersey number was perhaps a nod to the famous number 23. Wearing 24, he was above Jordan. The basketball world still mourns Bryant's tragic death. We are left with his shots, his smile, and his "Black Mamba" nickname.

That's what this book is all about – the flame of these champions will never be extinguished!

Rodolphe Gaudin

Young students on the women's basketball team at the beginning of the 20th century.

INTRODUCTION

THE BACKSTORY

Basketball can thank winter! The sport was created in December 1891 by James Naismith, a Canadian physical education and sports teacher working at the YMCA International Training School (now known as Springfield College) in Massachusetts.

Naismith was looking for an indoor sport to play during the winter to maintain physical fitness, but also to keep his students busy between the American football and baseball seasons. He was thinking of an activity with less contact than American football, to protect his students from injury.

BACK TO BASICS

On a rainy day, Naismith set up two fishing nets about 10 feet (3 m) off the ground, on either side of the gymnasium. Except, Naismith hadn't thought to remove the bottoms of the nets yet, so the ball had to be retrieved after each point scored. What he did do is establish five fundamental rules: the game is to be played with the hands only, with no possibility of concealing the ball, which must be large and light; running with the ball is forbidden, due to the cramped conditions of the gymnasiums and the need for self-control; shock contact is forbidden; any player may obtain the ball at any time; and finally, the goal is horizontal and high.

A few weeks later, James Naismith's original 13 rules of basketball were published in Springfield College's newspaper, *The Triangle*.

Here are the 13 rules, some of which are still relevant today:

1. The ball can be thrown in any direction with one or both hands.
2. The ball can be batted in any direction with the flat of the hand, with one or both hands, but never with the fist.
3. A player may not run while holding the ball. If they do, the player must throw the ball back from the place where it was caught. Allowance is made for a player who catches the ball while running at speed but tries to stop.
4. The ball must be held in or between the hands; the arms or any other part of the body must not be used to hold it.
5. No shouldering, holding, pushing, tripping, or striking an opponent in any way. The first violation of this rule counts as a foul, the second excludes the player from the court until the next goal, or even for the rest of the game, without being substituted, if the intention of the player committing the foul was to hit.
6. Striking the ball with the fist constitutes a foul, in accordance with articles 3 and 4; this foul is penalized in the same way as those described in article 5.
7. If one of the teams commits four consecutive fouls, a goal will be counted for the opponents (consecutive means without the other team committing any fouls).
8. A point is scored when the ball is thrown into the basket from the ground and remains there; this requires that those defending the goal do not touch the ball or prevent the goal from being scored. If the ball remains balanced on the edge of the basket and the defenders move the basket, the point is scored.
9. When the ball goes out of bounds, it must be returned to the court and played by the first player to touch it. In the event of a dispute, the umpire throws the ball back into the court. The player who throws the ball back into play has five seconds; if he exceeds this time limit, the ball changes sides. If a team deliberately holds up the ball to gain time, the umpire penalizes them with a foul.
10. The umpire will judge the players, note fouls, and notify the referee when three consecutive fouls have been committed. They can disqualify players in accordance with article 5.
11. The head referee judges the ball, decides whether the ball is in play, within the limits of the court, and to which side it belongs; they also monitor the time elapsed in the game. They decide whether a goal counts and keep track of the points scored, as well as carrying out the other duties usually assigned to a referee.
12. A game will last two 15-minute halves, with a five-minute break in between.
13. The team scoring the most points within this time will be declared the winner. In the event of a draw, and with the agreement of the captains, play may be extended until a new point is scored.

A player training on a basketball court in New York.

Kareem Abdul-Jabbar (33) of the Milwaukee Bucks.

The two-page document listing these 13 original rules was sold at auction in 2010 for $4.3 million.

The first public men's match took place in March 1892, between students from the YMCA International Training School and their teachers. The former beat the latter 5–1 in front of almost 200 spectators. The first women's match took place the following year, at Smith College in Northampton, Massachusetts.

The game quickly caught on, and was played at many American colleges. Basketball developed and the rules were refined. In 1897 the number of players per team was set at five.

IN THE OLYMPIC PANTHEON

In the late 1800s and early 1900s, foreign students who had studied in the United States began to spread basketball around the world. The sport crossed borders and even oceans. By this point, the fishing nets were replaced by metal hoops attached to panels.

The first European match was played as early as 1893 in Paris at the YMCA headquarters on rue de Trévise, where the world's oldest basketball court is located. It was also in Europe that the first international match took place in 1909, between Mayak Saint Petersburg (Russia) and an American YMCA team.

A few years later, in 1919, at the end of the First World War, the Inter-Allied Games organized in Joinville-le-Pont also helped make the sport even more popular. The United States won the final against France.

Michael Jordan (23) of the Chicago Bulls leaves the court after a playoff loss to the Milwaukee Bucks in 1985.

This event led to further development in both countries. The sport even caught the eye of the Olympic Committee.

The modern Olympics began in 1896 in Athens, and basketball was added as a demonstration sport at the third edition in St. Louis, Missouri, in 1904. Several tournaments were organized for the occasion, but it wasn't until the 1936 Berlin Games that basketball became an official men's sport. This was thanks to the creation, four years earlier, of the International Federation of Amateur Basketball (FIBA). Women's teams would have to wait until 1976 to participate in the Olympic Games.

THE NBA IS BORN!

Little by little, basketball began to take shape on both sides of the Atlantic. In 1898, the National Basketball League was founded; it was disbanded only six years later but was nevertheless the forerunner of the many professional leagues subsequently created in the

LeBron James during the Chicago Bulls-Miami Heat NBA game on February 21, 2013.

USA. Another league of the same name was created in 1937, merging in 1949 with the Basketball Association of America (BAA), founded in 1946, to become the National Basketball Association (NBA) as we know it today. The 1949–1950 season, won by the Minneapolis Lakers, is therefore considered the first in the history of the Big League, even though the three previous seasons under the banner of the BAA are included in the NBA's record books. The first stars arrived in the NBA in the 1950s and 1960s, with Wilt Chamberlain, Bill Russell, Oscar Robertson, and Jerry West, who gave his silhouette to the American league logo.

Kareem Abdul-Jabbar arrived in the 1970s; it was his star-power, and that of other players, that contributed to the great basketball boom of the 1980s. Increased worldwide broadcasting and the drama of feuds and drafts also drew in an international audience.

First Earvin "Magic" Johnson and Larry Bird clashed with their respective franchises, the Los Angeles Lakers and the Boston Celtics. Then, in 1984, Michael Jordan was drafted first overall and went on to revolutionize the sport over the next decade. Hakeem Olajuwon, John Stockton, Karl Malone, Patrick Ewing, Dominique Wilkins – to name but a few – also joined the NBA at the same time.

The rise of Michael Jordan in the 1990s united the NBA's audience and, above all, further popularized basketball worldwide. While the American league stands out for its level of play and appeal, many other leagues have managed to grow, mainly in Europe.

TOP: Boston Celtics logo at center court before Game 7 of the second round of the 2022 NBA Playoffs between the Boston Celtics and the Milwaukee Bucks at Boston's TD Garden, May 15, 2022.

BOTTOM: Los Angeles Lakers logo on the court at the Staples Center in Los Angeles.

Today, FIBA boasts over 450 million players worldwide. Countries in Asia such as the Philippines are also basketball obsessed, and in France, the French Basketball Federation (FFBB) had over 650,000 members in 2021/2022, making basketball the third most popular sport in the country, and the second most popular team sport behind soccer.

UNITED STATES

Kareem ABDUL-JABBAR

BORN ON: 16 April 1947

IN: Harlem, New York

HEIGHT: 7′2″ (2.18 m)

POSITION: Center

PROFESSIONAL CAREER: Milwaukee Bucks; Los Angeles Lakers

ACHIEVEMENTS: 6 NBA championships (1971, 1980, 1982, 1985, 1987, 1988); 6 NBA regular season MVP titles (1971, 1972, 1974, 1976, 1977, 1980); 2 NBA Finals MVP titles (1971, 1985)

Walt Bellamy (8) of the Atlanta Hawks tries to block Kareem Abdul-Jabbar (33) during the game at the Omni Coliseum in Atlanta, November 11, 1972.

His signature move was the stuff of legend. Kareem Abdul-Jabbar's majestic arm roll to the basket always turned a difficult situation in his team's favor. This famous skyhook has often been imitated but never equaled. It was at St. Jude's Elementary School, where he was the only Black kid in class, that the future center discovered basketball in the early 1960s. He was just 14 years old, but already 6 feet 9 inches (2.03 m) tall when he began to casually unleash dunks.

The orange ball became his source of inspiration. At Power Memorial Academy, Ferdinand Lewis Alcindor, as he was then known, put in a series of titanic training sessions. The work was relentless, but it got results. In his first game, the gangly teenager slammed home 56 points, then went on to rack up 71 straight victories with his university team.

On the family front, in the Inwood neighborhood in the heart of the Big Apple, "Lew" received a strict upbringing, based on dignity and honor. The child of immigrants from Trinidad and Tobago, Lew's police officer father was a stickler for discipline. He sent Lew to boarding school at Holy Providence in Philadelphia, where he was heckled by his classmates for his excellent grades. At 19, he moved to the West Coast and completed his studies in Los Angeles. Ultimately, he became the leader of the UCLA Bruins, coached by John Wooden, an icon of college sports in the United States.

ON THIS DAY . . .

APRIL 5, 1984
Place your bets! Right in the heart of Las Vegas, the jackpot city, Kareem Abdul-Jabbar made history on April 5, 1984. Against the Utah Jazz, the Lakers' center pulled off his famous skyhook with eight minutes left in the game. With this impressive move, the New York giant had just overtaken the scoring record of another US basketball god, Wilt Chamberlain, with a total of 31,422 points scored. An all-time NBA record! The court was then invaded by all his teammates, as well as the reporters and photographers who immortalized this incredible moment.

AN IRONCLAD MENTALITY

Lew Alcindor broke all the scoring records, then in a unique feat he became the National Collegiate Athletic Association's (NCAA) best player for three seasons. The governing bodies then decided to ban the use of the dunk under the basket at college level. This was a major blow for Lew, deprived of his favorite offensive weapon.

Lew was known for taking a stand off the court as well as on it. Already a civic activist, he refused to participate in the 1968 Olympic Games in Mexico City, protesting the racial segregation prevailing in American society. Despite his outstanding performances on the court, this decision caused quite a stir, and at away games, Lew was often criticized by some of the public. Around the same time, Lew turned down an offer of

Kareem Abdul-Jabbar of the Los Angeles Lakers on the court.

$1 million from the Harlem Globetrotters. He preferred to monetize his talent in the NBA, and in the 1969 draft, he opted for the Milwaukee Bucks.

On his first outings with the Bucks, Alcindor was reunited with an old acquaintance, Elvin Hayes, who had transferred to the San Diego Rockets. Nine years his senior, point guard Oscar Robertson pushed him to toughen up his game against visibly jealous opponents who were trying to unsettle him. "Lew," he said, "if you weren't so good, they wouldn't touch you!" In April 1971, the Bucks clinched the supreme title against the Baltimore Bullets, with a four-to-nothing sweep not seen since the Boston Celtics in 1959!

In a spiritual move, Lew Alcindor converted to Islam and, on May 1, 1971, became Kareem Abdul-Jabbar, a name that means "the noble servant of the Almighty." As in the case of the boxer Cassius Clay, later Muhammad Ali, the reception from basketball fans was frosty. Strong-willed, the giant faced pressure from all sides, even from the Black Muslim movement, which accused him of being too moderate and even threatened him physically. Abdul-Jabbar had to accept the protection of bodyguards.

From a sporting point of view, things were more rewarding. In 1974, for the first

DID YOU KNOW?

When little Joey, invited by the flight crew, enters the cockpit in the zany scene from the 1980 disaster-movie parody *Airplane!*, he is greeted by Kareem Abdul-Jabbar, playing co-pilot Roger Murdock.
The toddler recognizes him and calls out, "My dad says you don't work hard enough on defense and also that you tend to fall asleep on the court . . ." After pretending to be someone else, the irritated Lakers champion then grabs his young visitor by the collar for a completely absurd confrontation. Guaranteed to make you laugh!

Kareem Abdul-Jabbar of the Milwaukee Bucks in action against the Golden State Warriors during the 1972 season.

time, he was named in the NBA's top five defensive players of the season. What's more, his ability to extricate himself with ease from the backcourt, in a two-man situation, astounded spectators.

OFF TO LOS ANGELES

The following season, speculation was rife when Kareem Abdul-Jabbar announced his intention to leave Milwaukee. During a warm-up game, he fractured his hand while angrily punching a billboard after getting poked in the eye. To protect his damaged retinas, he was obliged to wear protective glasses, the famous goggles that would also become part of his legend. In June 1975, the contract was signed. Kareem Abdul-Jabbar, in exchange for Junior Bridgeman and Dave Meyers, joined the Los Angeles Lakers with his teammate Walt Wesley.

Even the arrival of Magic Johnson in the line-up wasn't enough to overshadow Abdul-Jabbar and, at age 33, the former Manhattan resident was still going strong. The Lakers' leading scorer, top interceptor, second-ranked passer, and second rebounder, he was still a force to be reckoned with. On June 13, 1989, playing against the Detroit Pistons at the Inglewood Forum, Kareem Abdul-Jabbar made one final leap, but the Michigan players didn't allow him the joy of completing a triumphant victory lap by winning the NBA Finals. In any case, nostalgic fans were already replaying the performances of an extremely elegant basketball player.

GREECE

Giannis ANTETOKOUNMPO

BORN ON: 6 December 1994

IN: Zografou, Athens

HEIGHT: 6'11" (2.11 m)

POSITION: Power forward/Center

PROFESSIONAL CAREER: Filathlitikos BC; Milwaukee Bucks

ACHIEVEMENTS: 1 NBA championship title (2021); 2 NBA regular season MVP titles (2019, 2020); 1 NBA Finals MVP title (2021)

Chicago Bulls' Tristan Thompson (3) tries to block the attack of the Milwaukee Bucks' Giannis Antetokounmpo (34) during the match at the United Center in Chicago, April 5, 2022.

Giannis Antetokounmpo didn't have any hoops installed in his garden. Bad move, as it was March 2020, and the Covid-19 pandemic had confined the entire planet. The basketball season came to a sudden halt. A blow for the power forward who, with a ferocious appetite for success, had been performing well in Milwaukee's line-up.

A TASTE OF REVENGE

Two years later, the Greek showed his teeth during a demonstration against the Brooklyn Nets, when he surpassed Kareem Abdul-Jabbar's 14,211 points to become the Bucks' all-time leading scorer. Nine seasons earlier, out of nowhere, Giannis had had the audacity to enter the NBA draft, even though no one knew his name. His motivation was to help his family financially. The unbelievable happened, as the Wisconsin franchise set its sights on the lad who had never set foot on an American court.

A month earlier, the future "Greek Freak" had obtained his Greek passport. The young man, of Nigerian origin, had no identity documents until 2013! As a teenager, he and his three brothers lived discreetly, selling counterfeit goods on the sly. Giannis grew up in Sepolia, a district in the north-west of Athens.

His parents had fled Lagos to try and survive in Europe. Their four children managed to survive, but the family name suffered the torments of translation. "Adetokunbo" became "Antetokounmpo" for the Athenian administration. Still, in his hometown, Giannis made a name for himself in a municipal gymnasium, where basketball became his real ally. And as soon as he earned his first salary in Wisconsin, he sent all the money he earned to his family in Greece.

His first NBA game was against the Bobcats when he was just 18 years old. Giannis used his robustness to hold his own against more experienced opponents. He is very agile, and his wingspan (7 feet, 7 inches, or 2.36m!) is extraordinary. He can easily pick up the ball with one hand, since each hand is no less than 13 inches (33 cm) in size, around the height of a water bottle.

DID YOU KNOW?

In August 2015, Giannis Antetokounmpo was summoned by Luol Deng, a former Bulls forward, to take part in a prestigious match in Johannesburg, South Africa. Team Africa took on Team World. Despite 22 points scored, the Greek Freak was unable to prevent his side's defeat (97–101). The goal of this event was to raise awareness of basketball among young Africans and encourage the NBA to invest in the continent by developing structures worthy of its name.

Constantly improving, the Greek Freak is increasingly explosive in transitions and brilliant on the block. He knows how to get out of complicated situations when isolated in a one-on-one and has never been so determined around the rim.

ADEPT AT THE SPECTACULAR DUNK

In January 2017, Giannis took part in his first All-Star Game with the Eastern Conference, alongside Paul George, Jimmy Butler, and LeBron James. At 22 years and 74 days, Antetokounmpo was the youngest Bucks player to be selected for this prestigious event. He scored 30 points, but his team lost to the Western conquerors (182–192). At the end of the season, he was voted April's Best Player of the Month. Insatiable, Giannis resumed the 2017–2018 season, with 147 points scored in the first four games, a feat not seen since Kareem Abdul-Jabbar in 1970–1971!

A perfectionist, the Greek power forward still has his doubts. "Every morning, I wake up anxious. I'm afraid I'm starting to think I don't need to work my ass off anymore!" And yet, in March 2019, he broke his NBA scoring record, with 52 cumulative units against the Philadelphia 76ers. Before claiming the ultimate title in 2021, Giannis extended his contract with the Bucks for the princely sum of $228 million over five years. Above and beyond his sporting achievements, the young Greek is proud to have helped his team get out of the rut they were in.

ON THIS DAY . . .

JULY 21, 2021

The date of July 21, 2021, will inevitably remain etched in Giannis Antetokounmpo's memory forever. That evening, at the Fiserv Forum, the Milwaukee Bucks snatched the decisive game (4–2) against the Phoenix Suns (105–98). An absolute title – their second in history – which had eluded them for 50 years! The Greek dominated both on defense and attack, scoring 50 points, with 14 rebounds and 5 blocks by the end.

Marcus Smart (36) of the Boston Celtics takes on Giannis Antetokounmpo (34) of the Milwaukee Bucks during the sixth game of the second round of the 2022 NBA Playoffs at the Fiserv Forum in Milwaukee, May 13, 2022.

UNITED STATES

Carmelo ANTHONY

BORN ON: 29 May 1984

IN: Brooklyn, New York

HEIGHT: 6'7" (2.01 m)

POSITION: Power forward

PROFESSIONAL CAREER: Denver Nuggets; New York Knicks; Oklahoma City Thunder; Houston Rockets; Portland Trail Blazers; Los Angeles Lakers

ACHIEVEMENTS: 3 Olympic gold medals (2008, 2012, 2016); 1 Olympic bronze medal (2004)

Carmelo Anthony (7) of the Los Angeles Lakers dribbles past Isaiah Joe (7) of the Philadelphia 76ers, at the Wells Fargo Center in Philadelphia, January 27, 2022.

For his big game, "Melo" pulled out all the stops. On March 12, 2017, the power forward remained focused, even though he was facing an opponent straight from his neighborhood: the Brooklyn Nets. Despite the emotion, Carmelo Anthony didn't make a fuss but calmly scored 27 points, securing a 120–112 victory for the Knicks. In doing so, he became the third player in NBA history to score over 10,000 points with two different franchises (Nuggets and Knicks), something only Kareem Abdul-Jabbar and Elvin Hayes had achieved before him.

ON THIS DAY . . .

AUGUST 21, 2016

On August 21, 2016, at the Carioca Arena in Rio de Janeiro, Carmelo Anthony, who scored 7 points in 17 minutes, became the only American player to win three Olympic gold medals in a row. Melo has also become the only NBA player to have participated in four successive Olympic Games since Athens in 2004. This is far from insignificant: the New York forward has joined the Olympic legend as the top American scorer, accumulating 293 points in total, 20 more than LeBron James.

POWER AND SPEED

Kobe Bryant had this to say about him: "Melo is a bull on the court!" Carmelo Anthony was indeed not easy to block and had a style that was difficult to figure out. Gifted at getting inside the paint, he often provoked the And-One (a successful shot, followed by a free throw after a foul). His whimsical side wasn't always appreciated – his tendency to play isolation ball was frustrating, and his lack of teamwork could be irritating. And for others, he was a killer, period!

Along with his siblings, Melo was raised by his single mother. As she worked as a cleaner, she wasn't often at home, but Mama Anthony encouraged the young Carmelo to stick with school.

In Brooklyn, Carmelo naturally turned to basketball. "You can find basketball courts on every street corner here," said the future NBA star. Later, he channeled his energy at Oak Hill Academy, a Virginia boarding school with ironclad discipline.

As a teenager, he bolstered the Syracuse Orange in the NCAA championship, leading them to the 2003 college title. Melo felt that the time had come to take things to the next level. A new horizon opened up for him when the Denver Nuggets signed him. Coincidence or not, at the end of the season, for the first time in 10 years, the Nuggets were back in the playoffs. The joy was short-lived as the Minnesota Timberwolves walked all over them, but Carmelo Anthony's career had finally launched.

A SETBACK

In the months that followed, "Mr. Clutch" – a reference to his ability to step up in the crunch time – racked up performances

averaging 26 points per game. And then, in December 2006 at Madison Square Garden, a brawl broke out with two minutes to go against the Knicks, his future destination. As everyone was calming down, Melo punched Mardy Collins in the face. As a result, the Nuggets forward was suspended for 15 games.

After the end of Anthony's suspension, Denver made the playoffs again but suffered another first-round defeat to the San Antonio Spurs. Melo then decided to concentrate on his game and ended the 2006–2007 season on a high note. With the Western Conference selection, "Melo Man" also took part in his first All-Star Game, scoring 20 points.

During the 2008–2009 season, everything fell into place, to the point where the Nuggets, the firm underdogs, finally reached the pinnacle of the NBA. However, after getting the better of the New Orleans Hornets and Dallas Mavericks, the series turned in favor of the Los Angeles Lakers (4 wins to 2), despite Carmelo Anthony being at the top of his game and formidable in the mid-range.

The end of the 2010 season was a turbulent one for Mr. Clutch, who refused to extend his contract with the Nuggets. On the lookout, quite a few franchises were in the running, but he remained in Colorado for more than six months.

Carmelo Anthony (15) during the NBA Playoff Conference Finals between the Los Angeles Lakers and the Denver Nuggets in Los Angeles, May 22, 2009.

Carmelo Anthony (00) of the Portland Trail Blazers grabs a rebound alongside teammate Hassan Whiteside (21) during a game against the New York Knicks at the Moda Center in Portland on December 10, 2019.

DID YOU KNOW?

"Oh my god!" This was the cry of astonishment from visitors. In 2012, basketball fans came to enjoy the wax statues at Madame Tussauds in New York, and discovered a statue of Carmelo Anthony. Except, on the day of the unveiling, it was the Knicks' forward himself, in the flesh, who was standing motionless. Hence the surprise when he came to life, in a fit of laughter, before shaking hands with all his fans.

BACK IN THE FOLD!

In February 2011, Melo joined the Knicks. From November to February, Carmelo Anthony played 31 games with 20 or more points, surpassing the previous record of former point guard Richie Guerin. On April 2, 2013, on the Miami Heat court, for the third time in his career, Anthony passed the 50-point mark, then racked up five games with 35 points or more, joining the legendary Wilt Chamberlain.

Anthony had knee surgery and went through a disastrous 2015–2016 season before getting back on his feet. But, after years of stability, the end of his career was marked by nonstop upheavals. A lackluster stint in Oklahoma City, an aborted transfer to the Atlanta Hawks, then a forgettable arrival with the Houston Rockets had all the fans doubting. Deemed too lax on defense, Carmelo Anthony tried to bounce back with the Chicago Bulls but, after some confusion, the deal fell through.

The forward was back on form in Portland, to the point of setting a new record on January 7, 2020, for the most shots made in the last five seconds of a game (17 in total). In the summer of 2021, the 37-year-old set himself yet another challenge by joining the Los Angeles Lakers. Having never won an NBA Final, Carmelo Anthony didn't back down: "I want to win this title, I don't care about the rest. That's the only thing on my mind!" Time was running out, but the New Yorker was at his best when the buzzer loomed.

UNITED STATES

Charles

BARKLEY

BORN ON: 20 February 1963

IN: Leeds, Alabama

HEIGHT: 6′6″ (1.98 m)

POSITION: Power forward

PROFESSIONAL CAREER: Philadelphia 76ers; Phoenix Suns; Houston Rockets

ACHIEVEMENTS: 2 Olympic gold medals (1992, 1996); 1 NBA regular season MVP title (1993)

Charles Barkley on the court after the USA's victory over Argentina at the 1996 Atlanta Olympic Games. He was awarded the title of his team's top scorer for his performance during the competition.

Despite Charles Wade Barkley's talent on the American courts, his list of achievements is not what it might have been. The Alabama power forward never managed to capture an NBA title.

Charles suffered from the utter frustration of never having worn the ring he wanted so badly. When he left the stage on April 19, 2000, for a final round of matches in his Houston Rockets jersey against the Vancouver Grizzlies, a staggering emptiness fell on his broad shoulders. Like a snapshot in time, symbolizing a dazzling career, "Chuck" rounded off his wild ride with a final basket scored after an offensive rebound.

ON THIS DAY . . .

NOVEMBER 7, 2002
From the commentary box, Charles Barkley was covering a Houston match alongside his former partner Kenny Smith. The former Rockets power forward declared that Yao Ming would never score more than 18 points in a game. "If he does it this season, I'll kiss Kenny's ass!" Chuck recklessly blurted out. Ten days later, the Chinese center scored 20 points and Charles Barkley had to honor his commitment. Smith sent him a donkey on the set of the show! The kiss on the animal's rump was fleeting but very real.

AN EXPLOSIVE CAREER

Having scored over 20,000 points, 10,000 rebounds, and 4,000 assists after 16 seasons at the highest level, "Sir Charles" joins other legendary all-rounders such as Kareem Abdul-Jabbar, Wilt Chamberlain, Tim Duncan, Kevin Garnett, LeBron James, and Karl Malone. A well-rounded player with an aggressive style, he was able to alternate between an attacking style, distributing the ball, and defensive shielding. His 24 triple-doubles (20 in the regular season, 4 in the playoffs, including 1 in the final) attest to his relentless performance. Capable of supersonic coast-to-coast runs, usually ending with a two-handed dunk, the double Olympic gold medalist had all the makings of a colossus.

Immune to pressure, Chuck was also sharper than most. Renowned for his trash talking, Barkley never minced words. Fans and media outlets reveled in his scathing sense of humor. It was unfiltered and too bad if the Southerner racked up the most fines in history due to misconduct.

ONCE UPON A TIME . . .

Legend has it that Charles Barkley was the first Black baby in a segregated state to be born in a maternity ward previously reserved for the wealthy whites. With an absent father and a mother remarried to a stepfather who died in a car accident when the boy was 11 years old, it doesn't take a rocket scientist to figure out that Chuck's childhood wasn't an easy one. All the more so since, while he discovered the joys of basketball in high

Charles Barkley (34) of the Phoenix Suns tries to recover the ball while surrounded by Dominique Wilkins (21) and Kevin Willis (42) of the Atlanta Hawks at the America West Arena in Phoenix, February 18, 1993.

school, his weight at 220 pounds (100 kg) became the subject of mockery. Called a "flying pig," the teased teenager took it all in his stride.

Tough but quick on his feet, Barkley was even named the 1984 NCAA Player of the Year, an ideal way to get into the draft, for which he was ranked fifth with the Philadelphia 76ers. Unfortunately, even though the rookie averaged 15 points per game, the Sixers lost their playoff title to the Boston Celtics.

Chuck's nickname "the Round Mound of Rebound" took on a new dimension the following season. The famous coach Pat Riley summed up Charles Barkley perfectly: "This guy is one of a kind. His exceptional muscles, dizzying speed, and steely mentality make him an extraordinary basketball player." During the 1987–1988 season, Julius Erving's retirement offered Barkley a leadership role with the Sixers. The cover of ***Sports Illustrated*** was recognition for him, a star who had emerged from the slums. Two seasons later, during the All-Star Game (he would go on to play in 10 in a row!), he led the Eastern Conference to victory (116–114), with 22 rebounds, a record previously set by Wilt Chamberlain in 1967.

BAD BOY

This big-hearted troublemaker went out of his way for a young girl who, having

Charles Barkley (34) of the Philadelphia 76ers in 1989.

DID YOU KNOW?

During the 1991–1992 season, Charles Barkley gave up his traditional number 34 to adorn himself with an unexpected number 32. A powerful symbol in support of Magic Johnson, who had just revealed his HIV-positive status.
However, for the Philadelphia 76ers, the number 32 was no longer worn on the roster, as a tribute to legendary forward Billy Cunningham. Still, inspired by Chuck's initiative, the Sixers' management agreed with his request and joined in support for the Los Angeles Lakers legend.

come to watch a match, unfortunately got hit with his spit, which was originally intended for a racist in the stands. To make amends, Chuck approached the family and offered seats, but a wind of disapproval nearly blew the undisciplined shooting star away. His arrival at the Phoenix Suns didn't soften his loud-mouthed nature, ready to fight over anything.

Nevertheless, Charles led the Arizona team to the NBA Finals, a first for the club since 1976.

However, Michael Jordan's Chicago remained a tough challenge for the Suns. In contrast to the bad boy image of his opponent, the Bulls' guard wanted to pay tribute to him . . . in his own way. "Charles is like your little brother. You feel like slapping him, but you love him anyway!"

From 1993 on, basketball's *enfant terrible* accumulated physical setbacks. Chronic back pain and repeated injuries made him question things. On the cusp of his 30th birthday, wasn't it time to retire from the US scene?

Although less regular, Charles Barkley still pulled a few explosive moves. Having just joined the Houston Rockets in 1996, he racked up 33 rebounds in his first game against his former franchise, the Phoenix Suns – a record for the Rockets! In November 1999, at the twilight of his professional career, Charles, surly and on the defensive, got into a heated argument in the middle of a match with Shaquille O'Neal. Like a brat, he was sent off by the referees. A month later, a ruptured left quad sealed Chuck's fate, forcing him to face the early downfall of a champion.

UNITED STATES

Elgin
BAYLOR

BORN ON: 16 September 1934 in Washington, DC

DIED ON: 22 March 2021 in Los Angeles

HEIGHT: 6'5" (1.96 m)

POSITION: Forward

PROFESSIONAL CAREER: Minneapolis Lakers; Los Angeles Lakers

ACHIEVEMENTS: NBA All-Star Game co-MVP (1959)

Signed photo of Elgin Baylor (22) from the cover of the Los Angeles Lakers' program on March 21, 1969, which became known as "Elgin Baylor Night."

When Elgin Baylor was growing up, there was nothing available to entertain him. Life was hard and humiliating. There was a recreation center near the farm where his family lived, not far from Washington, DC. However, due to America's racist segregation policies, Black people were not allowed to use it.

IN SEARCH OF IDENTITY AND RECOGNITION

Elgin and his two brothers, Kermit and Sal, had to make do on improvised courts. The obstacles to playing basketball continued at university because, despite Elgin's experience on high school courts, university teams did not recruit from Black schools in areas with segregation laws in place. The young forward did get a scholarship to the College of Idaho, but it was for him to play on the football team!

However, Elgin's talent broke down the walls of prejudice. His incredible one-handed shot astounded early observers, and they invited him to join the basketball team without even trying out. In 1958, Elgin left college to join the Minneapolis Lakers (the team would later move to Los Angeles). Effortless and perfectly agile, a true virtuoso with his aerial spirals, the rising star was at the top of the draft. However, the rookie was joining an aging franchise that lacked a dedicated venue. The team was far from popular and, to top it all off, in serious financial trouble. The owner, Bob Short, believed his new recruit would save the day for the ramshackle Minnesota team.

Nicknamed "the Rabbit" for his speed, Elgin finally felt respected, valued, and useful. Also known as "The Magnificent Loser," during his 13 seasons with the Lakers, Elgin Baylor played in eight NBA Finals but lost all of them! An anomaly in an otherwise incredible career.

Early in his career, Elgin was averaging over 30 points per game when the Lakers moved from Minneapolis to Los Angeles with the hope of a rebirth. Elgin's performances were intoxicating, and, thanks to his unique style, audiences discovered a previously unknown type of basketball. One of his most fierce competitors in the 1960s, the Boston Celtics' relentless center, Bill Russell, called Elgin the "godfather of suspended time." A true

ON THIS DAY . . .

JANUARY 16, 1959

On January 16, 1959, the Lakers traveled to Charleston, West Virginia, to face the Cincinnati Royals. The Kanawha Hotel, where the Californian players were to stay, refused access to its three Black players, including Elgin Baylor. The forward refused to take part in the game. To a teammate who tried to persuade him to play, he replied: "I'm a human being. I'm not an animal put in a cage and let out for the show."

pioneer in the game, the Lakers forward had enough creativity to maneuver with ease around a compact block and deftly dodge a defender's charge. "He was Jordan before Jordan," said Magic Johnson when he paid tribute to him.

THE FIRST HIGH-FLYING PLAYER IN THE NBA

In November 1960, the "Magnificent Loser" scored 71 points against the New York Knicks, an absolute record at the time. The following season, despite being called to military service and only joining his team on weekends as a reserve player, Baylor had a fantastic season.

Over the course of his career, Elgin Baylor would accumulate four games with more than 60 points. In April 1962, in the final against Bill Russell's Celtics, Elgin lit up Game 5 with 61 points, but the Lakers missed out on the ultimate title by losing the next two games. What followed was more painful. The Los Angeles players were always in the Celtics' shadow and, a victim of chronic knee problems, Elgin was losing momentum and no longer scoring more than 30 points in each game.

At the very beginning of the 1971–1972 season, Elgin ruptured his Achilles tendons, and after only nine games played, he decided to retire because of his injuries. In a cruel twist of fate, after Elgin's retirement the Lakers went on a 33-game winning streak, eventually winning the 1972 NBA Finals. The magnificent forward had never even gotten close to this Holy Grail. In a move that may seem trivial, the Californian officials offered the winner's ring to Elgin to show their gratitude to him for all that he had done for the team over the years.

Once his career was over, Elgin Baylor coached and managed teams from behind the scenes, never straying far from the basketball court. In 2006, he was awarded the NBA Executive of the Year trophy for his work. With the recognition of his peers, the former Lakers forward was at peace with his career. In 1977, he was also inducted into the US Basketball Hall of Fame, and his number 22 was immediately retired by the Lakers. With class and elegance, without fuss, like a star twinkling forever, Elgin Baylor crossed the threshold of immortality.

Elgin Baylor (22) of the Los Angeles Lakers in action against Bill Russell (6) of the Boston Celtics at the Los Angeles Sports Arena on January 1, 1966.

DID YOU KNOW?

In April 2018, Elgin Baylor was celebrated in front of the Staples Center in Los Angeles, the Lakers' home ground, with the unveiling of his statue. In the presence of Kareem Abdul-Jabbar, Shaquille O'Neal, Magic Johnson, and his longtime friend Jerry West, the Rabbit was deserving of such an honor. A video broadcast during the ceremony shows Kobe Bryant highlighting the exploits of his elder. "I want to thank you because I took so many moves from you," said the Black Mamba.

Larry BIRD

BORN ON: 7 December 1956

IN: West Baden Springs, Indiana

HEIGHT: 6'9" (2.06 m)

POSITION: Forward

PROFESSIONAL CAREER: Boston Celtics

ACHIEVEMENTS: 1 Olympic gold medal (1992); 3 NBA champion titles (1981,1984, 1986); 3 NBA regular season MVP titles (1984, 1985, 1986); 2 NBA Finals MVP titles (1984, 1986)

Lewis Lloyd (32) of the Houston Rockets shoots against Larry Bird (33) of the Boston Celtics during the 1986 NBA Finals at Summit in Houston, June 1, 1986.

In Game 6 for the 1981 NBA title, the Boston Celtics were in a bad position. They were trailing by 17 points. And then Larry Bird emerged. The Celts forward destroyed the Houston Rockets' backcourt in the final minutes and, largely due to his disruptive play, won the 14th trophy for his franchise, which was back in the spotlight after five years in the shadow.

A FARM BOY FROM INDIANA

DID YOU KNOW?

Twitter co-founder Biz Stone, a fan of the Boston Celtics, confirmed the rumor in 2011. The famous social network's logo, the blue bird, was indeed named Larry in honor of the legendary American forward.

A true all-around player, Larry Joe Bird was particularly formidable on the rebounds thanks to his sense of positioning. Beneath his clumsy exterior, the man nicknamed "Gold Hand" was terrifyingly skilled in the paint and beyond. Virtually ambidextrous, the famous number 33 even took pleasure in approaching certain matches by deciding to shoot only left-handed.

Larry never left a training session without making a series of perfect free throws, obsessing over the fact that the ball never touched the hoop. But in competition, his farm-boy physique frightened many. His looks matched his origins, and he couldn't distance himself from them. Growing up in French Lick, deep in southern Indiana, where there are more cattle than people, sums it all up. Little Larry had never seen a skyscraper. His world was the farm.

A young redhead with blue eyes, he also couldn't hide his Irish origins. It seemed as if his future destiny with the Celtics was already mapped out!

Larry grew up a baseball fan and had a blast with the bat at Springs Valley High School. It was only while watching one of his brother Mark's matches that things clicked. Joining the Hoosiers as soon as he entered Indiana University, the teenager achieved excellent performances under the basket. "I didn't have a plan," Larry recalled years later. "I never imagined I would one day play in the NBA!"

Rather than empowering him, with more than 30,000 students around him, campus life paralyzed him. Far from his hamlet of 2,300 souls, he felt suffocated. After a month, he packed up his college books and returned to his hometown. He settled for a job as a municipal agent and, even when mowing the lawn or collecting the trash, Larry felt less overwhelmed. In 1975, he pulled himself together and found his way back to college with

the Indiana State Sycamores, but had to wait until the start of the next school year before he could play there. And then, miracle of miracles, at not even 20 years old, Larry Bird was a hit in every area of the game!

In 1979, Larry took the leap into the unknown, with his NBA debut and a record contract for a rookie at $650,000 per season. Far from destabilizing him, the new Celtics forward became the leading scorer, and the Boston franchise took on a new dimension.

The 1981 title was the reward for a team with a wonderful style, in perfect harmony, and with masterful confidence. Like a fine wine, Larry Bird improved with time, and, when it came to the very special skill of free throws, Gold Hand was approaching a 90% success rate. With nerves of steel, the Celtics forward gained in confidence, to the point of joking around with teammates and opponents alike.

In February 1985, during a clash against the Utah Jazz, when he was flirting with perfect statistics, one of the assistants advised him to go for a quadruple-double. Larry replied: "What for? I've already done enough damage as it is!"

Larry Bird of the Boston Celtics in 1993.

From left to right: Pat Ewing, Larry Bird, and Michael Jordan.

ON THIS DAY . . .

MAY 5, 1981

This play has gone down in history. On May 5, 1981, during the NBA Finals against the Houston Rockets, Larry Bird pulled off a crazy move in the middle of Game 5. The Celtics' forward took a three-point shot, but felt that he was missing by a fraction of an inch. Number 33 anticipated the rebound on the hoop, caught the ball above the red scrum with his right hand and, still in the air, he brought the ball down with his left hand for a shot from nowhere! Victory 98-95 and a title in sight!

BETWEEN DREAM AND REALITY

After shocking everyone with his skill, Larry's injuries began. The cartilage of his right elbow was scattered like a jigsaw puzzle. Larry also suffered from a bad ankle and a bad right hand, but he never gave up. In 1986, he was even named MVP of the season for the third consecutive time – one of the only players to be so, along with Bill Russell and Wilt Chamberlain. Without a fight, the Houston Rockets were eaten alive in the final. The man nicknamed "the Hick from French Lick" destroyed the Rockets in mid-air with a triple-double.

The Celtics forward, who had surgery on bone growths on both heels in the summer of 1991, left his fans in awe. Despite suffering a concussion in the middle of a game, Larry was a true superman and set himself one last challenge. The International Federation had authorized pros to take part in the Olympic Games, with a view to the 1992 competitions in Barcelona.

And there he was, vice-captain of the Dream Team, shining alongside Magic Johnson, his former college rival. The US machine won gold, and Bird left the stage on that triumph. "Larry Legend" would continue to make a name for himself afterwards, becoming the first US basketball player to be named Best Executive of the Year 2012, thanks to his managerial involvement with the Indiana Pacers, the same team where he had been awarded MVP as a player and, later, as a coach. An unprecedented triple worthy of a lone cowboy who has become an icon in American sport.

UNITED STATES

Kobe
BRYANT

BORN ON: 23 August 1978 in Philadelphia, Pennsylvania

DIED ON: 26 January 2020 in Calabasas, California

HEIGHT: 6'6" (1.98 m)

POSITION: Shooting guard

PROFESSIONAL CAREER: Los Angeles Lakers

ACHIEVEMENTS: 2 Olympic gold medals (2008, 2012); 5 NBA championship titles (2000, 2001, 2002, 2009, 2010); 1 NBA regular season MVP title (2008); 2 NBA Finals MVP titles (2009, 2010)

Los Angeles Clippers' DeAndre Jordan tries to counter Los Angeles Lakers' Kobe Bryant (24) during an NBA game, April 7, 2013.

When the news of Kobe Bryant's death in a helicopter accident spread, a cloud of sorrow fell upon the world. Especially as the champion perished alongside his daughter Gianna, aged just 13. A cruel epilogue for a living god who until then had turned everything he touched into gold.

AN UNBREAKABLE MINDSET

ON THIS DAY . . .

JUNE 12, 2002
This was a first. At the age of 23, at the Meadowlands Arena in East Rutherford, near New York, Kobe Bryant had just won his third NBA title. The Los Angeles Lakers pulled off a memorable sweep (4 wins to 0), against the New Jersey Nets, by winning the decisive match (113–107). Never before has such a young player achieved such a performance on American courts.

On April 13, 2016, Kobe Bryant left the star-studded court with a legacy of 60 points scored against the Utah Jazz (101–96 victory). It was a sporting farewell for the former student of Philadelphia's Lower Merion High School, where the legendary shooting guard became first became a leading scorer. When it came to being drafted in 1996, Kobe Bryant was first chosen by the Charlotte Hornets, but Jerry West went out of his way to get the phenomenon. The Lakers manager bet everything on the gifted Pennsylvanian. At 17, Kobe went straight from high school to the NBA!

From his very first steps in Los Angeles, Kobe trained alone in the still darkened gym, before the arrival of the staff and his teammates. The Black Mamba was fine with this, and didn't mind putting himself at a disadvantage, aiming for the hoop in the dark.

Still capable of improvement, Kobe impressed with his initiative, even if he was far from being successful in everything. And then, his already-magical duo with Shaquille O'Neal was bliss.

A cold-blooded animal in his shots, his nickname – linked to the snake with its venomous bite – is not at all unreasonable. As a striking example, he would never leave a training session until he had hit the net 400 times! What's more, we often forget that Bryant was an impressive defender in the NBA, notably achieving 1,944 interceptions – an absolute record for the Lakers! In the 1999–2000 season, at the top of his game, Kobe, in total levitation, conquered his first title.

CHAMPION IN EVERY CATEGORY

At the beginning of 2002, Kobe Bryant shone like never before at the All-Star Game in his beloved Philadelphia and was voted

MVP. The young man was all the more fulfilled as he married Vanessa Laine, with whom he would have four daughters. On the basketball front, with Shaquille O'Neal injured, Kobe struggled to keep the Lakers at the top of the pyramid. Still, he notably scored more than 40 points in nine straight games.

During the following season, everyone had sky-high expectations. But the first cracks appeared in the middle of the flashy picture. Kobe was accused of egocentricity, and tensions appeared between him and Shaquille O'Neal, whom Kobe judged as "lazy."

Salary-driven, Kobe was reported to be leaving for the Clippers, but in the end, it was Shaq who set sail for Miami. On Christmas Day 2004, the two men came face-to-face in the Lakers-Heat clash and, despite Kobe's 42 points, it was his former accomplice who came out on top. Criticism continued to rain down, with some of the Black Mamba's teammates ordering him to stop his permanent one-man show. Two years later, Kobe Bryant gave up his usual jersey with the number 8 for the number 24. For the record, he's the only player in NBA history whose two numbers have been retired by his franchise, in this case the Lakers.

Shaquille O'Neal (34) of the Los Angeles Lakers chats with teammates Kobe Bryant (8) and Ron Harper (4) during a timeout against the Indiana Pacers during the NBA Finals at Canseco Fieldhouse in Indianapolis, June 1, 2000.

Kobe Bryant (24) during an NBA game between the Los Angeles Lakers and Oklahoma City Thunder on December 19, 2014.

DID YOU KNOW?

If you lived in the Haut-Rhin region of France in 1992, you may have unknowingly come across 13-year-old Kobe Bryant! But what was the future NBA star doing in the heart of Alsace? His father Joe "Jelly Bean" Bryant was also a professional basketball player. After seven seasons in Italy, he ended his career that season at FC Mulhouse Basket in eastern France. At the end of the season, the legendary nomad returned to Philadelphia, Pennsylvania.

GAME OVER . . .

Despite the criticisms, on January 22, 2006, Kobe slammed 81 points against the Toronto Raptors (122–104). More dominant than ever, Bryant achieved the NBA double in 2009 and 2010 and went on to achieve the same feat with the Dream Team, two-time Olympic gold medalists in 2008 and 2012. In December 2012, Kobe Bryant passed the symbolic milestone of 30,000 points since his NBA debut 16 years earlier.

Five months later, against the Golden State Warriors, Kobe came to an abrupt stop: struck down by a ruptured Achilles tendon, the Black Mamba was down for the count. At 34, the horizon seemed to be darkening, but the Lakers' guard negotiated a new contract for an additional two years. He returned in December 2013 but fractured his knee. Bad luck continued to dog him and, after tearing his right shoulder, he retired in April 2016.

With five NBA titles, 1,346 games played, and a grand total of 33,643 points scored, Kobe Bryant was inducted into the US Basketball Hall of Fame at a posthumous ceremony in February 2021. Supported by Michael Jordan, Kobe's wife Vanessa paid tribute to her hero husband. "I'm sure he's laughing in heaven because I'm about to congratulate him," his lifelong love still found the ability to joke. An emotional and nostalgic audience was humbled by the power and simplicity of the message. Even today, on certain evenings, the Black Mamba can be seen twirling above the courts.

UNITED STATES

Jimmy

BUTLER

BORN ON: 14 September 1989

IN: Houston, Texas

HEIGHT: 6'7" (2.01 m)

POSITION: Shooting guard/Forward

PROFESSIONAL CAREER: Chicago Bulls; Minnesota Timberwolves; Philadelphia 76ers; Miami Heat; Golden State Warriors

ACHIEVEMENTS: 1 Olympic gold medal (2016); 1 NBA MIP title (2015)

Jimmy Butler (21) of the Chicago Bulls drives to the basket against Arron Afflalo (10) of the Denver Nuggets during a game at the Pepsi Center in Denver, November 25, 2014.

For once, luck wasn't against him. It was the middle of summer 2012 and, taking advantage of Luol Deng's injury, Jimmy Butler was given a starting position as forward for the Chicago Bulls. It had been a year since the Texan had joined the team, but he'd only played snippets of matches. This time around, Jimmy took the opportunity to pull out all the stops. With over 20 points per game, the Houston native's career was finally taking off.

ON THIS DAY . . .

FEBRUARY 11, 2021

A repeat offender if ever there was one, on February 11, 2021, Jimmy Butler pulled off his 10th triple-double in the NBA against the Houston Rockets with 27 points, 107 rebounds, and 10 assists, for a Miami victory (101–94). On January 24, 2022, he did it again, this time with his 10th triple-double in a Heat jersey (18 points, 10 rebounds, and 12 assists), beating the previous record of LeBron James with the Florida franchise. Mission accomplished against the Los Angeles Lakers (113–107) led by . . . LeBron James!

LIFE WAS A BATTLE

Butler's early years on the streets of his suburb played out like a caricatured film noir. An absent father. A mother who, when Jimmy had just turned 13, threw him out of the house.

Jimmy lived from day to day, like a stray dog. Every day, he improvised, staying with the parents of friends who were affected by his story. Not wanting to be a burden, he moved homes almost every night. And then, at 17, he met a basketball player friend, Jordan Leslie.

The two never left each other's side. Aware of his situation, Jordan's parents, despite their modest income, ended up accepting Jimmy into their home. He became their eighth child.

At the same time, he enrolled at Tyler Junior College and was already dreaming of the NBA. In 2008, with his budding talent, Jimmy moved to Marquette University in Wisconsin. Jimmy's coach made a point of instilling in him the basics of the game. Still a chrysalis, the butterfly in the making was puny and needed to grow his athletic wings.

Jimmy's efforts paid off, and at the 2011 draft, it was time to take flight. Few franchises were willing to bet on Jimmy with his unorthodox style and quirky shot, but he was finally drafted by the Bulls. Confined to the mission of being the back-up to the back-up, far behind Carlos Boozer and Luol Deng, the young forward or shooting guard – depending on who you ask – bided his time. As fate would have it, Deng was out, and Jimmy was now scraping by under the NBA hoops. He exploded during the 2014–2015 season and America discovered a surprisingly mature novice.

Jimmy Butler (22) of the Miami Heat dunks during the seventh game of the 2022 Eastern Conference Finals against the Boston Celtics at Miami's FTX Arena, May 29, 2022.

SHARP AND HANGING ON

Jimmy plays the old-fashioned way, certainly not impressive in terms of scoring, but his hustle is a blessing. In May 2015, he won his first individual award, named NBA Most Improved Player – the first Bulls player to receive this title.

The following season, Butler extended his contract in Chicago and, mentally liberated, broke his scoring record in January 2016, against the Sixers, with 53 units. He went on to finish the Rio Games on the top step of the Olympic podium.

Months went by and Jimmy became a key figure in the US basketball landscape. Even a meniscus operation in February 2018, when he joined the Minnesota Timberwolves, did not distract fans from the fierce backcourt player he is, even if a few eager critics accused him of selfishness.

The uneasiness increased in the summer of 2018 when, after surgery on his right hand, Butler refused a contract extension with the Timberwolves. He instead asked for a transfer, and when he returned to the paint in the fall, there was a lot of grumbling in the stands of the Target Center. It's not always easy

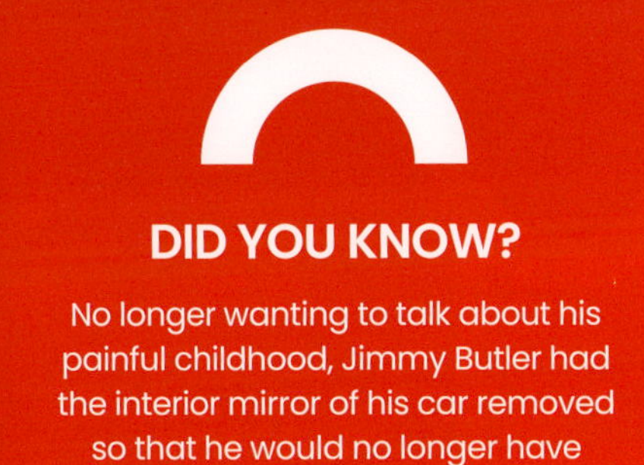

DID YOU KNOW?

No longer wanting to talk about his painful childhood, Jimmy Butler had the interior mirror of his car removed so that he would no longer have to look back! With this aversion to pointless sentimentality, Jimmy had this to say: "When I started to make my breakthrough, that's all anyone could talk to me about. If I get stuck in my own history, I won't move forward. I've moved on from the hard times, but I don't hold any grudges." Making a clean sweep of the past is part of his perpetual fight against injustice.

Jimmy Butler (22) of the Miami Heat takes a shot against the Philadelphia 76ers during the sixth game of the second round of the 2022 NBA Playoffs at the Wells Fargo Center in Philadelphia, May 12, 2022.

to follow Jimmy's career logic, as he frequently changes his mind. Finally, in November, Jimmy Butler joined the Philadelphia Sixers. But eight months later, the small forward signed a four-year contract with the Miami Heat.

MIAMI HERE WE COME!

Feeling liberated in Miami, Jimmy put in one stellar performance after another. Between a record for rebounds and qualifying for the 2019 NBA Finals, everything seemed to be going his way. But LeBron James' Lakers were unsinkable in the finals. The Heat paid dearly for the absences of the injured Bam Adebayo and Goran Dragić. Jimmy Butler put his guts on the line in the first make-or-break matches but, worn out by his top-class performances in which he went above and beyond, he physically cracked in Game 6, leaving the title to the Lakers.

Showing resilience, outcast Jimmy didn't give up. He packed up, headed west, and went back into battle. "I learned from the best," he said in one of the few media interviews he gave. "My teammates taught me how to play and how to become a man." A no-nonsense doctrine. And some would have us believe that Jimmy Butler, a child from nowhere, a star in his later years, is just selfish? A specialist in intercepting, Butler is always there for the rebound.

In February 2024, Jimmy Butler was traded to the Golden State Warriors. At 35, he was taking on a new challenge alongside franchise star Stephen Curry. Butler chose No. 10 as his jersey number to pay homage to Paul Pogba and Neymar.

UNITED STATES

Wilt CHAMBERLAIN

BORN ON: 21 August 1936 in Philadelphia, Pennsylvania

DIED ON: 12 October 1999 in Los Angeles, California

HEIGHT: 7'1" (2.16 m)

POSITION: Center

PROFESSIONAL CAREER: Harlem Globetrotters; Philadelphia Warriors; San Francisco Warriors; Philadelphia 76ers; Los Angeles Lakers

ACHIEVEMENTS: 2 NBA championship titles (1967, 1972); 4 NBA MVP titles (1960, 1966, 1967, 1968)

Wilt Chamberlain (13) of the Philadelphia 76ers takes a shot against Mel Counts (31) of the Los Angeles Lakers at the Los Angeles Memorial Sports Arena.

On April 24, 1967, Wilt Chamberlain's ultimate dream came true. At the age of 30, the Philadelphia 76ers center finally won his first NBA title. During Game 6 in the final, the Sixers stunned the Warriors (125–122) and planted their flag at the pinnacle of American basketball.

FIRST STEPS WITH THE HARLEM GLOBETROTTERS

Throughout his career, Chamberlain collected more than 70 all-round records. But, before climbing to the top of his game, Wilt was still labeled a loser since, for eight seasons, he never managed to finish a season triumphantly. Despite this "second-place syndrome," the center from Pennsylvania popularized moves that have since become legendary, such as his signature arm roll. He also pioneered the dunk and the finger roll, moves he learned in his early professional days.

Wilton Norman Chamberlain might never have become an exceptional champion, as he suffered from pneumonia as a child. To recover from this, the future Goliath became a star on the athletics track. On his 10th birthday, he was already over 5 feet, 9 inches (1.80 m) tall and quickly realized that basketball was for him. At Haddington Recreation Center and then at Shoemaker College, Wilt continued to grow. At 15, his height of 6 foot 8 (2.10 m) was intimidating.

In 1953, "Wilt the Stilt" – a nickname he never appreciated – was still a school high-jump champion. But at 17, he enrolled at the University of Kansas and played with the Jayhawks. In his first game with the Jayhawks, the newcomer was impressive, scoring 52 points and 31 rebounds.

After two years at the collegiate level, Wilt felt he was stagnating and set his sights higher. However, he was still too young to join the NBA. So, in 1956, he joined the Harlem Globetrotters. Three years later, the president of the Warriors, convinced that he'd made the right choice, bet everything on this slight but incredibly effective player.

Not one to follow the crowd, Wilt had no qualms about taking the number 13, which is generally avoided out of superstition. He didn't care; his jersey number didn't stop him from averaging 30 points a game. At 7 feet 1 inch (2.16 m) tall, Wilt towered over

DID YOU KNOW?

The challenge seemed completely impossible. In 1971, Wilt Chamberlain contacted the boxing legend Muhammad Ali to propose a face-off in the ring. After negotiations and the promise of a hefty sum, a date was announced for the fight – July 26. After a meeting on a TV set, where he was intimidated by Ali's provocations, Wilt the Stilt seemed overwhelmed by what was at stake and ended up canceling his incredibly bold challenge.

the court. His fluidity was fascinating and his flexibility allowed him to dodge his opponents' shots. Despite his physical potential, the young center was always a generous team player.

MEETING AT THE TOP

On October 24, 1959, at Madison Square Garden, Wilt Chamberlain played the very first of his 1,045 NBA matches, scoring 43 points and 28 rebounds against the New York Knickerbockers (118–109). The captivated audience also witnessed his first dunks. In his fourth game, he had his first encounter with Bill Russell, his counterpart at the Boston Celtics. Clashes of titans would become his daily bread. Exposed to all kinds of knocks during the regular season, the "Big Dipper" lost two teeth and then fractured his knuckles. Voted rookie of the season, despite serious hardships, Chamberlain already had eight records in his trophy cabinet.

The Philadelphia giant was so talented that the NBA introduced new rules, such as banning him from taking a jump on free throws or blocking a ball on its way down. At the start of the 1962–1963 season, the Warriors moved from Philadelphia to San Francisco, but that didn't stop Wilt from regularly finishing games with more than 70 points.

In the 1964 off-season, Wilt accepted the Philadelphia 76ers' contract to return home. All would have been well if that damn Bill Russell hadn't blocked his path to the final in a nail-biting finish. Tired of being considered a graceful loser, Wilt Chamberlain demanded more defensive intensity from the Sixers, even if it meant losing his reputation as the best scorer. He wanted the title at all costs and didn't care if his team lost its pride. The gamble paid off in that blessed year of 1967, and the center was finally able to put on the much-coveted ring.

He repeated the feat five years later with the Los Angeles Lakers and his magical Elgin Baylor-Jerry West duo. Despite his physical decline, Chamberlain remained determined. In the 1971–1972 season, the Lakers racked up 33 consecutive victories and entered the record books. In February, Wilt became the first player to score 30,000 points in the NBA. Despite the fame, Wilt was worn down by the endless traveling and his chronic insomnia. He decided to step down. He passed away from heart failure in October 1999, aged just 63.

ON THIS DAY . . .

MARCH 2, 1963
There is no better way to cement your place in history. On March 2, 1963, the Warriors hosted the New York Knicks. In a white-hot arena, Wilt Chamberlain reached the mythical 100-point mark in a single game. On their feet in the game's final moments, the audience screamed hysterically: "Give it to Wilt!" The feat was accomplished with 46 seconds to go. Fans invaded the court. It was never really known if the game had been finished. In April 2000, the match ball was sold at auction for over $550,000!

Wilt Chamberlain (13) of the Los Angeles Lakers tries to block Kareem Abdul-Jabbar (33) of the Milwaukee Bucks.

UNITED STATES

Stephen CURRY

BORN ON: 14 March 1988

IN: Akron, Ohio

HEIGHT: 6'2" (1.88 m)

POSITION: Point guard

PROFESSIONAL CAREER: Golden State Warriors

ACHIEVEMENTS: 2 World Championship titles (2010, 2014); 1 Olympic gold medal (2024); 4 NBA Championship titles (2015, 2017, 2018, 2022); 2 NBA regular season MVP titles (2015, 2016); 1 NBA Finals MVP title (2022); NBA All-Star Game MVP (2022, 2025); 1 NBA Citizenship Award (2023)

Stephen Curry (30) of the Golden State Warriors grabs the rebound against the Boston Celtics during the sixth game of the 2022 NBA Finals at TD Garden in Boston on June 16, 2022.

In May 2019, in the Conference Finals against Portland, Stephen Curry made life miserable for the Trail Blazers. With his Golden State Warriors team, the point guard scored 146 points in just four games, an absolute record in a sweep against the opponent. Considered the best shooter of all time, "the Baby-Faced Assassin" has a unique ability to shoot effortlessly. With such astonishing coordination and fluidity of movement, his exceptionally flexible wrist does the rest.

ON THIS DAY . . .

MAY 10, 2016

On May 10, 2016, for the first time in NBA history, a player was unanimously chosen as MVP by 131 voters. Stephen Curry scored 1,310 points out of a possible 1,310! More than Shaquille O'Neal in 2000 and LeBron James in 2013, who had both missed the perfect score by just one vote. Behind the Warriors' point guard, the San Antonio Spurs forward, Kawhi Leonard, settled for an unremarkable second place, with 634 points.

FROM UNSPECTACULAR BEGINNINGS . . .

Stephen's reputation as a brilliant sharpshooter on three-point shots speaks for itself. For five seasons, from 2013 to 2017, Curry was at the top of the list of the specialists in this skill. Yet at 15, he wasn't the most talented of the bunch. In the paint, he was the king of missed shots. His father Dell, a shooting guard with the Charlotte Hornets, decided to take his clumsy son under his wing. Stephen was determined to follow in his father's footsteps.

Being so small, the young man didn't impress anyone and didn't win any scholarships to the most reputable colleges. He had to settle for a less prestigious college, Davidson. But this didn't stop him from becoming the top scorer in the NCAA for three seasons.

Eventually, Wardell (his real name!) Stephen Curry started to get noticed. In the 2009 draft, the Golden State Warriors snapped up the baby-faced prodigy. While on an individual level Stephen made a good debut, from a collective point of view, it was less convincing. The Warriors were struggling in terms of results. Stephen Curry's 2011–2012 season was a long, hard road. He suffered a torn ankle ligament and underwent surgery twice in the space of six months. The following season was one of rebirth, and the arrival of rookie Klay Thompson was an absolute blessing in disguise. The two young ambitious Warriors got on well together, and Stephen took on the leadership role with the poise of an old hand.

SHOWBIZ INSTINCT

Everything came together in 2013–2014. Curry broke Ray Allen's record for three-pointers (272 vs. 269) and the Oakland franchise returned to the playoffs after a six-year absence. Sure, the San Antonio Spurs were the stronger team, but Curry lit up the game and delighted fans with his showmanship, not to mention his risk-taking. During the next part of the season, the arrival of coach Steve Kerr saw Curry move up another notch in the hierarchy. First, Golden State had a historic season with an 81 percent-win rate, and at age 26, "Baby Face" was now a key figure in the NBA.

In May 2015, Stephen was named MVP of the season, beating out James Harden and LeBron James. The latter said: "I love this guy. It's best to guard him as soon as he gets out of his car to enter the building." In any case, Stephen was the first player to lift this trophy for the Warriors since Wilt Chamberlain in 1960. In the playoffs against the Memphis Grizzlies, this crafty player shattered the three-point shot record, previously held by Reggie Miller. And to top it all off, Golden State won the ultimate title for the first time since 1975, following a 4–2 win against the Cleveland Cavaliers.

Backed by an outstanding Kevin Durant, Curry went on a rampage in the

Stephen Curry (30) gets the better of Luka Dončić (77).

finals against the Cleveland Cavaliers to win the second ring of his career. Despite the excitement, Stephen broke tradition and, with his teammates' agreement, he refused to celebrate the victory at the White House, in protest of Donald Trump's policies. Unheard of in Washington!

Stephen Curry (30) of the Golden State Warriors moves towards the basket to block Kris Humphries (43) and Brook Lopez (11) of the Brooklyn Nets during a game at the Oracle Arena in Oakland on November 21, 2012.

WELL DONE, MAESTRO!

Despite a stubborn ankle the following year, Stephen played a remake of the previous lineup. The final against the unhinged Cavaliers was a mere hiccup and the Warriors won their third championship in four years. Things got complicated over the next few months. The combined injuries of Kevin Durant and Klay Thompson were too debilitating. Despite his brilliance, Stephen Curry couldn't save Golden State in the final and left the title to the Toronto Raptors. After the gloomy Covid period, the Warriors' point guard was back on track. In January 2021, he broke his scoring record against Portland, with 62 points.

Between Christmas and New Year's Day, the "Baby-Faced Assassin" smashed the NBA three-point shooting record, with a dizzying total of 3,000 long-range baskets. Although it would be simplistic to limit Curry's talent to this one feat alone, the statistic is striking. Even the league's highest-ranking officials were stunned, as was NBA commissioner Adam Silver: "Stephen has revolutionized the way basketball is played and continues to leave fans in awe with his amazing artistry and extraordinary shooting ability." You never get tired of it.

DID YOU KNOW?

Suffering from a genetic eye disease, Stephen Curry has had blurred vision since childhood. He has keratoconus, an inflammation of the cornea that blurs his vision in bright light. "I started wearing contact lenses," the Warriors point guard said. It is not uncommon to see photos of him squinting to aim when firing a shot. In the United States, some commentators were quick to say, "Luckily he doesn't see perfectly!"

Luol

DENG

BORN ON: 16 April 1985

IN: Wau, Sudan

HEIGHT: 6'9" (2.06 m)

POSITION: Forward

PROFESSIONAL CAREER: Chicago Bulls; Cleveland Cavaliers; Miami Heat; Los Angeles Lakers; Minnesota Timberwolves

ACHIEVEMENTS: 1 NBA Citizenship Award (2014)

Chicago Bulls' Luol Deng (9) drives against the Dallas Mavericks during the fourth quarter at the United Center in Chicago on January 20, 2011. The Bulls won 82–77.

Born in the town of Wau, in what is now South Sudan, Luol Deng didn't always see basketball as a priority in his life. Like many of his fellow citizens, he was a victim of the country's civil war, and the Deng family had to flee the deadly conflict to Egypt. However, his father was arrested there, and his mother was left to support the nine children on her own. An escape from this cramped life in a tiny apartment was soon found – basketball. While they were in Egypt, Luol and his siblings had met Manute Bol, the Sudanese-American former NBA player. This chance encounter inspired Luol and his brothers to play basketball. Even today, Luol never hesitates to recall the importance that the late Bol had in his life. And his life was about to change radically. His father was granted political asylum, and the family was able to move to London, where they enjoyed much better living conditions.

ON THIS DAY . . .

FEBRUARY 26, 2012
Luol Deng has always wanted to highlight his African roots. In 2012, when he was selected for the All-Star Game, he decided to break the dress code to reveal a T-shirt featuring a design of his native continent. It was a powerful gesture in a very formal league, aimed at inspiring as many young African people as possible and giving them hope. He later explained his intentions behind this action: "I didn't want the kids to just see it and walk by. I wanted them to remember where I came from and take something away from it."

MANUTE BOL AS HIS GUIDE, THE BULLS AS HIS FAMILY

Once in England, Luol fell in love with soccer and the Arsenal FC, but he soon had to make a choice between soccer and basketball. It was a choice that was quickly guided by his height. Standing at 6 foot 8, the courts were the obvious choice. Playing against other teens, he excelled and joined the junior national team, with whom he competed in the FIBA Europe Under-18 Championship qualifiers. Averaging 40 points and 14 rebounds, the trial was a success, and Deng could imagine a future with the sport.

During that famous Euro, he continued his impressive performances and caught the eye of an American scout, who mentioned a scholarship and the Blair Academy in New Jersey. At the age of 14, Luol moved to a fourth country, but this time he was alone, far from his family. Deng wanted to work twice as hard to prove himself. And it paid off! In the United States, he was one of the best high school players in the country, and very quickly, the doors of renowned NCAA programs opened up for him. That's how the forward ended up at Duke, one of the best teams in history.

In one year at Duke University, Deng averaged about 15 points and 7 rebounds a game, with impressive three-point shooting.

Luol Deng of the Miami Heat makes a drive through the New York defense, slicing his way to the basket on November 30, 2014, at Madison Square Garden in New York.

His profile was a perfect fit for the NBA. After a detour to the Final Four of March Madness, Luol entered the big league when he was selected seventh overall by the Phoenix Suns, who immediately traded him to the Bulls. Luol's story was starting to sound like a fairy tale, and he found a second family in Chicago. With 11.7 points per game and already notable defensive skills, Luol Deng was named to the NBA All-Rookie First Team. Most importantly, Chicago qualified for the playoffs for the first time since 1998 and the Bulls' last title.

Deng was in his element in the NBA. A hard-working, behind-the-scenes player, he made steady progress, and Chicago began to look good again, with three

consecutive postseason appearances. One of the best perimeter defenders in the league, Luol also focused on scoring and consistently scored around 15 points per game as a key member of the starting five.

Named to the All-Star Game in 2012 and 2013, Luol Deng was now an established player in the league and a valuable trade asset. His defense and scoring reliability, complemented by one or two stars, made him a coveted veteran. Then he began his tour of the country. In 2014, after 10 years in Illinois, he was traded to the Cavaliers, before leaving for Miami for two seasons. As a free agent, he then signed with the Lakers and visited Minnesota and the Wolves. Never crowned champion, he failed in his quest for the title but left behind the image of a team player, a strong defender, and a hard worker, who was also capable of scoring, with a career high of 40 points in 2007. Symbolically, it was in Chicago that he signed his last contract in 2019. A symbolic agreement, as he did not play, it nevertheless allowed him to leave the world of basketball as a Bulls player.

ALL FOR AFRICA

Dedicated to the team throughout his career, Luol Deng is also a man who never forgets where he came from. Just a few months after his retirement in 2019, Luol was appointed president of the South Sudan Basketball Federation. South Sudan had only achieved its independence in 2011, but that didn't stop Deng from striving to put his country on the African and even global basketball map. This includes participation in the 2024 Paris Olympics and the 2023 World Cup in Indonesia, Japan, and the Philippines. The country even won its first-ever game in the competition at both tournaments. South Sudan has become the first African country to win a basketball game at the Olympics since 1996, while also achieving the best result for a nation from the continent at the World Cup!

Luol Deng is genuinely the driving force behind Sout. Sudanese basketball. For several years, he has financed most of the national team's expenses, such as hotels, travel costs, infrastructure, and everything else necessary for the development of the Bright Stars. He also played a key role in recruiting to the national team's coaching staff a former high school teammate, Royal Ivey, who played in the NBA for 10 years and then spent nine years as an assistant coach. Luol deserves just as much credit for bringing in NBA players such as Wenyen Gabriel, whose experience lifts the whole team and makes the South Sudanese project a real success story. Both on and off the court, Luol Deng continues to win everyone over.

DID YOU KNOW?

Luol is not only a representative of Sudan, and the NBA understands this well. Launched in 2020, the BAL, or Basketball Africa League, is designed to bring together the best teams on the continent. As the league grows at breakneck speed and the players have become increasingly strong, Luol Deng is naturally involved in its development as an ambassador. This is further proof of his commitment to nurturing basketball in Africa.

SLOVENIA

Luka DONČIĆ

BORN ON: 28 February 1999

IN: Ljubljana

HEIGHT: 6′6″ (1.98 m)

POSITION: Shooting/ Point guard

PROFESSIONAL CAREER: Real Madrid Baloncesto; Dallas Mavericks; Los Angeles Lakers

ACHIEVEMENTS: 1 Euro Championship title (2017); 1 EuroLeague title (2018); 3 Spanish league titles (2015, 2016, 2018); 2 Copa del Rey wins (2016, 2017); 1 Intercontinental Cup win (2015)

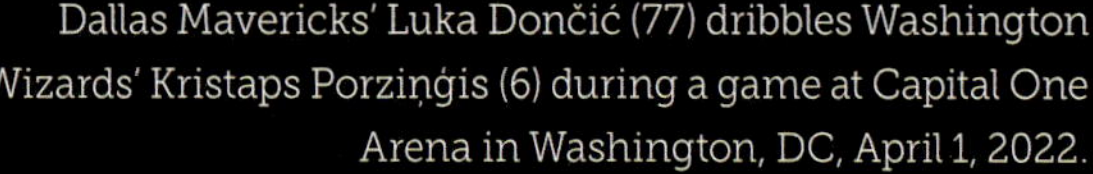

Dallas Mavericks' Luka Dončić (77) dribbles Washington Wizards' Kristaps Porziņģis (6) during a game at Capital One Arena in Washington, DC, April 1, 2022.

ON THIS DAY . . .

MAY 20, 2018

The crowning glory on May 20, 2018! At the Kombank Arena in Belgrade, Real Madrid won its 10th EuroLeague in its history, defeating Turkey's Fenerbahçe (85–80) in the final. Luka Dončić was named best player of this grand final and, as usual, best under-22-year-old player of the game. To top it all off, the talented Slovenian was also crowned MVP of the Final Four, which was held in the Serbian capital. Throughout the season, the phenomenon averaged 16 points per game.

From the moment he began playing, he amazed his coaches. Luka Dončić was only eight years old, but he was born to play basketball. Highly gifted, Luka was immediately promoted to the higher youth categories, but because of local regulations, he could not compete in the older age groups. So instead, he would go and watch his teammates' performances in order to analyze them.

"As a child," said Luka, "I had to find ways to beat stronger opponents by compensating with technique." And he did just that. In February 2012, at just 13 years old, he joined the ranks of the prestigious Real Madrid Baloncesto. "The Wonder Boy" was the youngest Real Madrid player to take part in the Minicopa Endesa. This Spanish youth tournament is reserved for future stars, and Luka managed to shine so bright that he was named best player of the tournament.

Six months later, the Slovenian sensation signed a five-year contract with Real Madrid, where he was two years younger than his teammates. Nevertheless, in a clash against Barcelona, nothing phased him and he racked up 25 points, 16 rebounds, and 5 steals. With Luka Dončić, nothing is ever mundane. His basketball IQ is off the charts and he leaves many people speechless with his ability to unhinge opposing defenses with ease.

On April 30, 2015, he made his debut with Real's flagship team against Málaga, and even the star of the moment, forward Felipe Reyes, was spellbound. Barely two minutes on the court and Luka had scored his first three-point basket in the Liga! The following season, he became a regular in Madrid's legendary big five. In January 2016, it almost bordered on arrogance. After a time-out against CSKA Moscow, "El Matador," as he was already known, scored three consecutive three-pointers in less than two minutes.

AN ARTIST WITH A LASER-BEAM PASS

Naturally, the Spanish and Serbian federations wanted to get their hands on the prodigy, but in September 2016, Luka Dončić declared his allegiance to Slovenia. A year later, his dream came true. Slovenia triumphed at the Euro, dominating neighboring Serbia in the final in Istanbul (93–85). Despite a performance hampered by a battered knee, Luka's first triumph on the continental stage will go down in history.

During the 2017–2018 season, Luka became even more crucial at Real, especially after Sergio Llull's serious injury. In March 2018, in a symbolic move against Red Star Belgrade, the club of his childhood dreams, Luka won for his team at the buzzer with a final three-point basket (82-79). In the Spanish league, Luka Dončić was naturally named MVP, earning a spot on the season's best team. On June 21, 2018, the shooting guard took it to another level. Having arrived in third position in the American draft, he was now in the sights of the Atlanta Hawks but joined the Dallas Mavericks in exchange for US point guard Trae Young.

Team Slovenia's Luka Dončić (77) is blocked by Team France's Nicolas Batum (5) during the men's basketball semifinal game at the Tokyo 2020 Summer Olympics at the Saitama Super Arena.

Due to a late departure from Real Madrid, he didn't make his NBA debut until four months later, against the Phoenix Suns, with 10 points, 8 rebounds, and 4 assists. Two weeks later, Luka finished his first American game with over 30 points against the San Antonio Spurs. He was already voted Rookie of the Month in the Western Conference! "He's not afraid of anything. He's fearless. You don't see that every day," said Rick Carlisle, his coach at the Texan club.

In January 2019, Luka Dončić became the youngest player in NBA history to record a triple-double, with 30 points scored against the Milwaukee Bucks, surpassing LeBron James in terms of prodigious ability.

Luka Dončić at the Real Madrid-Unicaja Málaga match, January 24, 2016.

DID YOU KNOW?

For his arrival in the NBA with the Dallas Mavericks in the fall of 2018, Luka Dončić had the badge honor of playing the entire season with Dirk Nowitzki, who, at 40 years old, was about to end his professional career. The legendary German forward even tested the young virtuoso during the first training sessions, challenging him in an attempt to destabilize him. The Slovenian kid smiled at him before successfully converting the two free throws he had just been awarded – without even faltering. A stunned Nowitzki said: "Luka is so far ahead of his years that it's scary!"

MIND-BLOWING STATISTICS

The following month, Wonder Boy passed the 1,000-point mark in the NBA before his 20th birthday. Then he went on to break Magic Johnson's record for achieving a third triple-double at such a young age, beating the American star by 117 days. At the end of the season, he was named Best Rookie of the Year, becoming the second European, after Spain's Pau Gasol, to win the title. In January 2020, Luka became the youngest basketball player from Europe to take part in the All-Star Game and, the following month, he became the youngest player to break the 300 three-pointers barrier before the age of 21. What more can we say?

Despite a bitter first playoff experience in August 2020, Luka extended his contract with the Mavericks for five years. Luka knew he was talented, but as he matured as a player, he was also determined to become more composed. Long considered unbearable due to outrageous behavior towards referees and even his teammates ("He's always barking," say his detractors), Luka was trying to mend his ways.

"The way I acted was unacceptable," he acknowledged. "It's over now! I had a little chat with myself . . ." The surprising key to his new mental approach: the once-aspiring singer began to hum a few tunes as therapy. Just to avoid any wrong notes from now on.

On February 1, 2025, he was traded to the Los Angeles Lakers, a sensational trade with Anthony Davis, who was making the opposite move.

UNITED STATES

Tim DUNCAN

BORN ON: 25 April 25 1976

IN: Saint Croix, US Virgin Islands

HEIGHT: 6'11" (2.11 m)

POSITION: Power forward

PROFESSIONAL CAREER: San Antonio Spurs

ACHIEVEMENTS: 5 NBA championship titles (1999, 2003, 2005, 2007, 2014); 2 NBA regular season MVP titles (2002, 2003); 3 NBA Finals MVP titles (1999, 2003, 2005); 1 Olympic bronze medal (2004)

San Antonio Spurs' Tim Duncan (21) drives to the basket against Washington Wizards' Brendan Haywood (33) at the Verizon Center in Washington on January 2, 2010.

Tim Duncan should perhaps never have landed on the bench of a franchise that had never won an NBA title. It was 1997, and the power forward out of Wake Forest University was causing a stir among US basketball fans, all the while excelling in his college psychology program. Promised the top spot in the draft, Duncan had just put in four full seasons in North Carolina and was attracting interest from all over the Big League. Led by David Robinson, the San Antonio Spurs were one of the best teams in the country. Except that, injured for most of the 1996–1997 season, Robinson had let San Antonio sink for a year. It was enough to finish with a record of 20 wins and 62 losses, securing them the first pick! While the team regained its leader the following season, the Texas franchise also found a way to give him a worthy partner in the paint – Tim Duncan.

Rookie of the Year Duncan, who then formed the "Twin Towers" with Robinson, experienced the joys of the playoffs in his first season, before winning his first title the following year. Overpowering in the paint, the Spurs crushed the finals, giving the Wolves, Lakers, Blazers, and Knicks no chance. At the age of 23, Duncan was already an NBA champion and even voted Finals MVP, with an average of 27 points, 14 rebounds, and 2 blocks per game.

DID YOU KNOW?

Before dominating the courts, Tim Duncan was destined for the swimming pools. One of his country's great hopes in the sport, Tim saw a hurricane hit the US Virgin Islands in 1989, destroying the only Olympic swimming pool there. While his sister Tricia had competed in the 1988 Olympics, Tim's dream was shattered by having to train in the middle of the ocean. The problem was that Duncan was scared to death of sharks, so lost his desire to train and gradually gave up swimming. He would return to the Olympics a few years later, but unfortunately for him, it was the fiasco of Athens 2004 . . .

POP, ROB, GINO, AND TP

Truth be told, Tim Duncan exceeded expectations. He was head and shoulders above the competition. He won two MVP titles (in 2002 and 2003) and put together one dominating season after another. In 19 NBA seasons, he was selected for the All-Star game 15 times. In his first eight years, he averaged over 20 points each time, peaking at 25 in 2001–2002, when double-doubles were his trademark (1,005 in 1,643 games). But more importantly, the Spurs built around him the foundations of what would become one of the best teams of the 21st century.

In 1999, the Spurs drafted Manu Ginóbili and in 2001, Tony Parker. With these two, Tim Duncan formed a formidable "Big Three" for over a decade, helping the Texans to put an end to the Lakers' dynasty, champions from 2000 to 2002. Duncan was at the center of the action and continued to torment opposing

Tim Duncan (21) of the San Antonio Spurs soaring through the air against the New Orleans Hornets during an NBA game in the New Orleans Arena on January 18, 2010.

THE MAN OF FUNDAMENTALS

Before becoming one of the best basketball players in history, Tim Duncan built his career with a contrasting style to modern NBA players. Nicknamed "the Big Fundamental," the power forward was a far cry from the ultra-spectacular players seen on today's courts. Quiet and sometimes described as boring off the court, Tim was a player who relied above all on the fundamentals of his sport. Setting the right screen, getting the rebound right, playing high

defenses. With the Frenchman and the Argentine, San Antonio had a fabulous trio, which the power forward enhanced. So much so, that according to Shaquille O'Neal, Tim was even "the best in history" at his position. An opinion shared by many, even if the Spurs went through a dry spell and didn't return to the NBA Finals until 2013.

ON THIS DAY . . .

JUNE 15, 2003

On June 15, 2003, the New Jersey Nets looked like children lost in the big leagues. The Nets were the verge of losing the NBA Finals against the Spurs, trailing 3–2, and Tim Duncan looked set to seal the deal in no time at all. That evening the two-time MVP power forward delivered one of the greatest individual performances in playoff history to hand the title to the Texans. He racked up 21 points, 20 rebounds, 10 assists, and 8 blocks! Two points shy of a quadruple-double and a playoff record, Duncan clinched the title and the Finals MVP trophy, and gave his teammate David Robinson, who was retiring shortly thereafter, a fitting farewell gift.

Tim Duncan (21) of the San Antonio Spurs in action against the Chicago Bulls on March 20, 2008.

or low post with his positioning skills, or even his legendary mid-range shot off the backboard. Why try to shoot the ball directly into the hoop, with a more random success rate, when you know the secrets of the backboard by heart? With his shot off the backboard, Duncan shut down more than one NBA defense and earned himself a perfect shooting spot for his entire career. He had mastered every aspect of the game in the paint, to the point where he was virtually unplayable when he got into position. His game was far from "flashy," but it was incredibly consistent, earning him praise from Kobe Bryant in 2014: "I can't emphasize how jealous I am of him." Most of all, Kobe understood the intensity of Tim's desire to win. "He's a quiet competitor. I'm much more demonstrative. But he has the same fire inside him as I do."

At the height of his 26,496 career points, 15,091 rebounds, and 3,020 blocks, Tim Duncan retired without fanfare or a farewell tour on July 11, 2016. In 19 seasons with just one franchise, he accumulated 19 playoff campaigns and became the only player in history to start for a championship team in three different decades. In between some MMA sessions with his buddy David Robinson, and a stint as assistant coach on the Spurs bench, Duncan enjoys a well-deserved retirement. His number 21 is now retired in Wake Forest and San Antonio, and he has, of course, entered the NBA Hall of Fame on the first try. With his simple style, Tim Duncan ended up winning everyone over.

UNITED STATES

Kevin DURANT

BORN ON: 29 September 1988

IN: Washington, DC

HEIGHT: 6'11" (2.11 m)

POSITION: Forward/ Power forward

PROFESSIONAL CAREER: Seattle SuperSonics; Oklahoma City Thunder; Golden State Warriors; Brooklyn Nets; Phoenix Suns; Houston Rockets

ACHIEVEMENTS: 4 Olympic gold medals (2012, 2016, 2021, 2024); 1 World Championship title (2010); 2 NBA Championship titles (2017, 2018); 2 NBA Finals MVP titles (2017, 2018); 1 NBA regular season MVP title (2014)

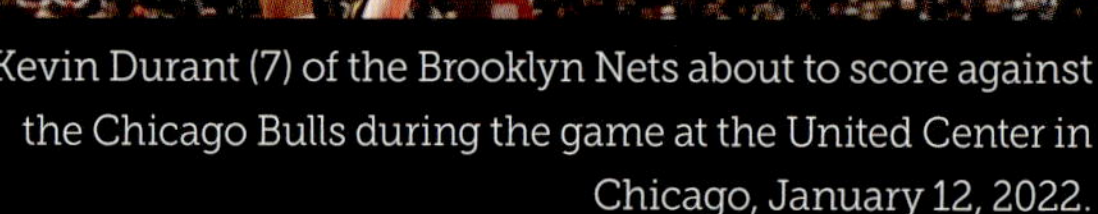

Kevin Durant (7) of the Brooklyn Nets about to score against the Chicago Bulls during the game at the United Center in Chicago, January 12, 2022.

Fed up with his comfort zone, Kevin Durant left Oklahoma City in July 2016. He signed a golden contract with the Golden State Warriors, with the overriding challenge of winning the ultimate prize, the NBA title. He achieved this at the end of the season, winning the trophy in the final against Cleveland. The forward would repeat this success the following season against the same Cavaliers.

THE BEST KIND OF MODERN BASKETBALL PLAYER

Some followers criticized KD's choice, suspecting that he had chosen the "easy" option by joining the most successful franchise at the time. A simplistic and narrow-minded opinion, especially since Kevin Durant won the honorary but highly coveted title of Most Valuable Player on two occasions. Impressive in driving to the hoop, quick despite his height, and a specialist at drawing fouls, he also has few equals when it comes to mid-range shooting.

Raised with his older brother Tony by his grandmother in Seat Pleasant, in the heart of Suitland, Maryland, Kevin was left without a father, who had abandoned the family home. In fact, for his sporting career, the American forward chose the surname of his mother, Wanda Durant.

Kevin discovered basketball at the age of 11, playing for the Prince George Jaguars in his native Maryland. Three years later, he began to line his bedroom shelves with his first trophies and told his mother he wanted to play in the NBA. Then KD continued to rack up more awards, this time at university, and as proof of his burgeoning fame he was nicknamed "Green Room" – the term for the room where future draft candidates wait off-stage.

ON THE FRONT PAGE

Crowned as the best college player, Kevin Durant found himself facing a league that was reaching out to him. Especially the Seattle SuperSonics, who, in the summer of 2007, got their hands on the genius from Suitland.

Voted rookie of the season, Kevin adapted without hesitation and became an indispensable cog in the wheel. Nothing could

ON THIS DAY . . .

APRIL 11, 2016

Impressive long-term statistics for a champion at this level. On April 11, 2016, Kevin Durant broke an incredible record at the Chesapeake Energy Arena. With 34 points to his name, the Oklahoma City Thunder power forward was one of the key players in the significant victory over the Los Angeles Lakers (112–79). This is the 64th consecutive time that KD has broken the 20-point barrier in a match. He then overtook his opponent for the evening, Kobe Bryant, who had set the previous record in the 2005–2006 season.

stop him, not even the fact that his franchise moved and changed its identity, becoming the Oklahoma City Thunder. An excellent rebounder, Kevin improved in defensive play with each game.

In February 2012, for the first time, Kevin scored more than 50 points against the Denver Nuggets. What's more, for his third All-Star Game appearance he was named Most Valuable Player. This was rounded off by a brilliant run in the playoffs, with major wins over the Mavericks, Lakers, and Spurs. Over 300 million Americans were eagerly awaiting the final showdown between the world's two best players, LeBron James on one side and Kevin Durant on the other. But LeBron's Miami Heat was untouchable.

Still, the insatiable Kevin Durant kept up the pace and, in November, at just 24 years old, he reached the symbolic milestone of 10,000 NBA points! Two years later, he broke Michael Jordan's record of 41 consecutive games with more than 25 points per game. Voted MVP at the end of the regular season, he lost his swagger, and, with his success flagging, was no longer a threat to the Memphis Grizzlies.

THE TROUBLE CONTINUES . . .

In the 2014–2015 season, Kevin Durant fractured his right foot, missing around 20 games at first. His physical pain dragged out for several weeks before he threw in the towel in March 2015, with the hope of coming back stronger. This happened in the 2018–2019 season, during which the phenomenal forward played 78 games, averaging 26 points per game. He became the most consistent player for the Golden State Warriors, which he joined two seasons earlier, achieving the success we're all familiar with.

Unexpectedly, things then went wrong in the playoffs. Already suffering from a torn calf, KD ruptured his Achilles tendon in the finals against the Toronto Raptors. Come summer, the Maryland basketball player became a free agent and eventually joined former Boston Celtics point guard Kyrie Irving in Brooklyn. As if to ward off bad luck, he abandoned his traditional jersey number 35 for number 7.

This was a false start, however, as Kevin was hit by the coronavirus in March 2020, and didn't play his first game with the Nets until nine months later. At the age of 30, Kevin Durant continued to set records, such as the 48 points he scored

Kevin Durant (35) of the Oklahoma City Thunder dunks during the game against the Dallas Mavericks at the American Airlines Center in Dallas, January 2, 2012.

DID YOU KNOW?

This almost became a national affair in the United States. For several months, NBA statisticians fought tooth and nail to find out Kevin Durant's true height! The mystery remained unsolved for a long time. "When I talk to women, I'm 6 foot 11. In basketball, 6 foot 8 is enough," he joked. KD did his utmost to cover his tracks, before his franchise announced that its number 7 was officially 6'11" (2.11 m).

in a decisive Playoff Game 7 against the Milwaukee Bucks, and the 25,000 points he reached in March 2022 in the regular season. In April, as casually as anything, Durant scored 55 points against the Atlanta Hawks. It goes to show that he can do whatever he wants – as a child, he imagined himself as a weather presenter on television. Instead of commenting on weather forecast maps on TV, however, the clever Washingtonian launched his own basketball collection with his gear sponsor, stamped "KD 6 Meteorology." Enough to soar above the clouds.

On July 6, 2025, the NBA made Kevin Durant's trade official. He left the Phoenix Suns to join the Houston Rockets. Durant thus became the face of the Rockets' renaissance. His immediate future promises to be strategic and decisive for the franchise.

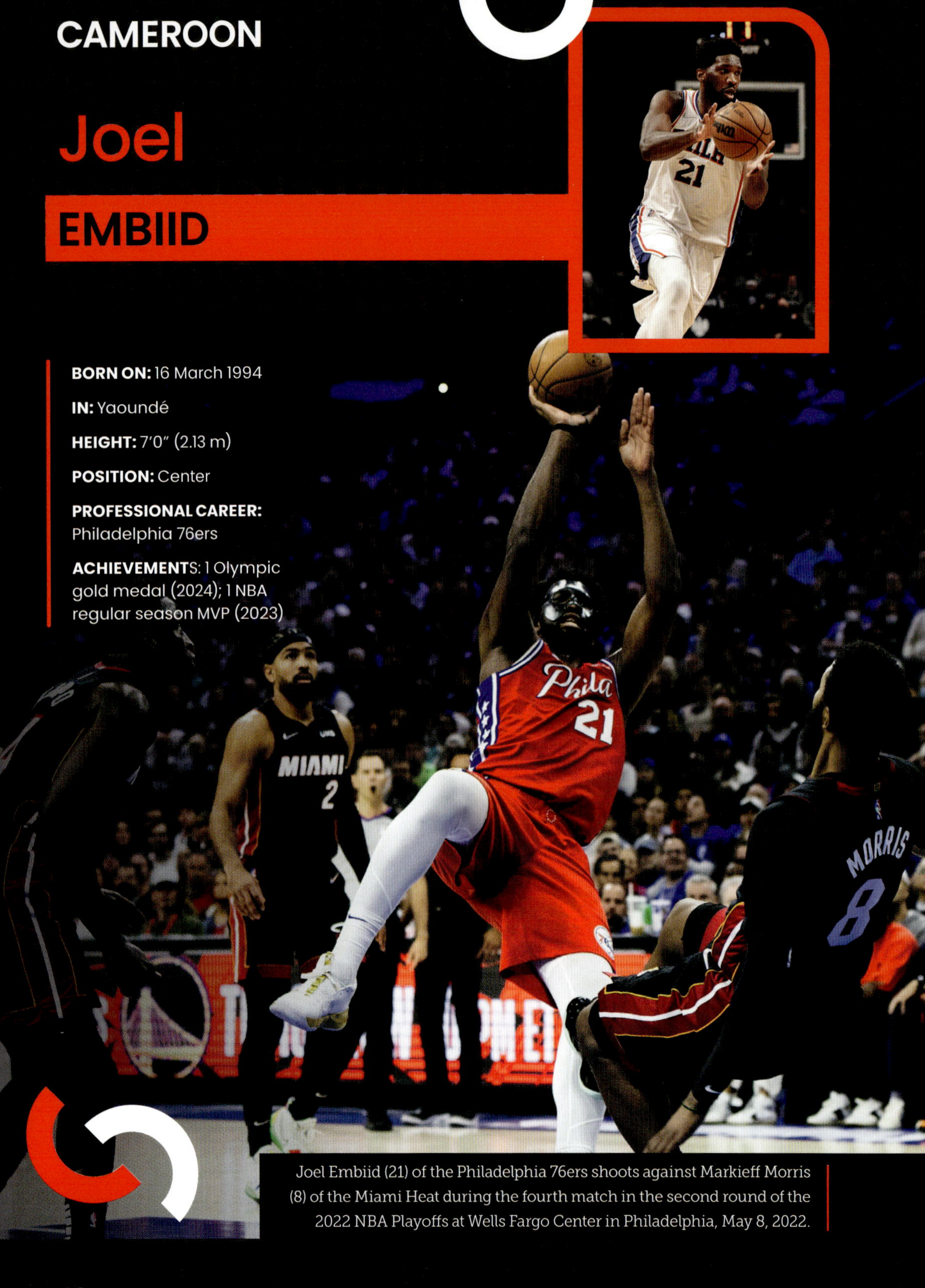

CAMEROON

Joel EMBIID

BORN ON: 16 March 1994

IN: Yaoundé

HEIGHT: 7′0″ (2.13 m)

POSITION: Center

PROFESSIONAL CAREER: Philadelphia 76ers

ACHIEVEMENTS: 1 Olympic gold medal (2024); 1 NBA regular season MVP (2023)

Joel Embiid (21) of the Philadelphia 76ers shoots against Markieff Morris (8) of the Miami Heat during the fourth match in the second round of the 2022 NBA Playoffs at Wells Fargo Center in Philadelphia, May 8, 2022.

"His opponents think they can throw him off his game, but he proves them wrong. If you 'trap' Jo, he'll make you pay!" This comment comes from Doc Rivers, coach of the Philadelphia 76ers, and perfectly sums up the level Joel Embiid has reached in the NBA today. The Cameroonian has made enormous progress on hedging, containing drives, and sliding, and his mobility allows him to maximize his offensive impact. Through hard work, "the Process" – a nickname linked to a Sixers' fan chant – is considered a true basketball quarterback.

ON THIS DAY . . .

MAY 2, 2022

The news came like a shockwave. On May 2, 2022, Joel Embiid made an official request to obtain French nationality. Rumors quickly took on proportions that went beyond basketball. And the French team's general manager, Boris Diaw, admitted that these steps had been taken to ensure that Joel could join Les Bleus in the near future. The goal – Paris 2024!

A MATTER OF PHYSICAL FITNESS

Over the last two seasons, "JoJo" has been able to eradicate one of his main weaknesses: a lack of muscle. It must be said that, with frequent visits to the health clinic, the young man had an often-disrupted start to his career. Foot, back, ankles, hands, wrists – everything on his medical record was flaring up at a frenetic pace. Having undergone surgery for a stress fracture in his foot in June 2014, this serious NBA contender was spending a lot of time in rehab.

Joel was originally spotted on the courts by Milwaukee Bucks and Sacramento Kings forward and fellow Yaoundé native Luc Mbah a Moute, who encouraged him to make the move to the US. Joel's parents had dreamed of him becoming a doctor, but with Luc's mentorship he became committed to playing professional basketball. A true godfather, Luc helped Joel get into his alma mater Montverde Academy in Florida. Joel had a great time at various universities, where he made his mark on the courts, before finishing his studies in style at the University of Kansas.

By January 2014, he was at the top of the draft, an essential springboard to the NBA. Unfortunately, JoJo was stuck in the NCAA due to his physical setbacks. His value was inevitably dropping with most franchises, and the opportunity seemed to be slipping away for good. Despite this, the Philadelphia 76ers dared to bet on the slightly built player who had spent so much time either stuck in bed or brooding over his frustrating bad luck.

THE MEANING OF THE GAME

After months of struggling, on October 27, 2016, Joel Embiid finally saw the light at the end of the tunnel, with his unforgettable NBA debut against Oklahoma City Thunder. Despite the Sixers' defeat (97–103), the young center did rather well, with 20 points on the counter, plus 7 rebounds, all in 22 minutes. The rookie was one of the season's pleasant surprises. And as luck finally seemed to be on his side, he even took part in his first All-Star Game in 2018.

A year later, Joel stunned spectators with a near-record 20 out of 21 free throws against Boston. A skilled shooter, the Process is also effective at containing opposing attacks. Thanks to his XXL wingspan, this big guy is a defensive wall and, more importantly, he's a sharp playmaker. As the Sixers' number 21, Joel Embiid made an exception for a match against the Golden State Warriors in January 2020, donning jersey 24 in tribute to Kobe Bryant. The Lakers guard had just passed away and the Cameroonian had lost one of his idols. The blow was especially painful as he had already lost his younger brother Arthur, aged 13, in a car accident in Yaoundé.

In the league, JoJo's talent was on display every time he took to the court and, in February 2021, against the Bulls, he broke his scoring record, with 50 points to his name. He became the NBA's top scorer, averaging 30.6 points per game, a first for a non-American player. He is also the first center to achieve such a feat since Shaquille O'Neal in the 1999–2000 season.

INDESTRUCTIBLE

Caught off guard by bad luck, Joel tore a ligament in his right thumb just as the Sixers qualified for the playoffs. Despite the pain, the Process hung on, opting for an operation in the off-season. But the bad luck persisted. After a duel against the Miami Heat, he suffered a blow to the head and fractured his frontal bone! The indestructible Cameroonian returned as soon as possible and, courageously, worked twice as hard in raining.

DID YOU KNOW?

In the land of the Indomitable Lions, like all Cameroonian children, Joel Embiid was a soccer fan, but also a volleyball fan. In fact, Joel's father would have liked to see his son make it in Europe through this sport, like many of their fellow countrymen. Until the age of 15, JoJo showed great aptitude for performing at the net, with quality blocks and some technical moves borrowed from a certain Earvin Ngapeth, the tricolor and world volleyball star of Cameroonian origin. In the end, Joel chose basketball!

Joel Embiid (21) of the Philadelphia 76ers blocked by Ayo Dosunmu (12) of the Chicago Bulls during the game at Wells Fargo Center in Philadelphia, March 7, 2022.

A real hype element in the second part of the 2021–2022 season, the Sixers center put in some first-rate performances. Given the potential of this determined player, some former champions, despite their genuine admiration, want more from him and are quick to criticize his tendency to lose focus and get rattled on the court whenever things don't go his way.

JoJo sees these words as a source of encouragement: "I think it's positive for me. I have the potential to become the best player in the world, but I know I've only partially shown it." Frustrated by his playoff failure against the Miami Heat in May 2022, Joel Embiid knows that he'll have to work hard, calm his temper, and get even more involved to take his franchise to the top. And he hopes that his physique holds up. "I'm going to keep pushing myself," said the Process, determined not to just go through the motions in certain games anymore.

However, tensions in the Sixers locker room and a nightmare 2025 season could lead him to leave the franchise.

UNITED STATES

Kevin GARNETT

BORN ON: 19 May 1976

IN: Greenville, South Carolina

HEIGHT: 6'11" (2.11 m)

POSITION: Power forward

PROFESSIONAL CAREER: Minnesota Timberwolves; Boston Celtics; Brooklyn Nets; Minnesota Timberwolves

ACHIEVEMENTS: 1 NBA championship title (2008); 1 NBA regular season MVP title (2004); 1 Olympic gold medal (2000); 1 NBA Citizenship Award (2006)

Boston Celtics' Kevin Garnett (5) tries to pass despite pressure from Toronto Raptor's Chris Bosh (4) in Toronto on November 23, 2008.

"Anything is possible!" This phrase, shouted towards the ceiling of Boston's TD Garden on championship night, is perhaps the most memorable image of Kevin Garnett in the NBA. Finally crowned champion after 13 years of failure, Garnett could finally celebrate a long-awaited accomplishment.

OUT OF HIGH SCHOOL AND INTO THE NBA

Unlike the vast majority of NBA players, Kevin Garnett never set foot on an NCAA court or played in any other professional league before joining the NBA. Drafted fifth overall in 1995, he made the leap straight out of high school, graduating from Farragut Academy, as his academic results were not good enough to get him into college. A consummate professional, he had no trouble fitting into the NBA and making a name for himself through steady progress in his early years. In fact, he got off to an idyllic start. He quickly became the mainstay of the team, earning him the nickname "Big Ticket," partly because he was credited with bringing the crowd back to the stands in Minnesota, a franchise that had long been struggling.

Between 1997 and 2003, he even led the Timberwolves to seven consecutive playoff appearances. Unfortunately, each one ended the same way – elimination in the first round. MVP of the 2003–2004 season, which he played in its entirety, with 24 points, 14 rebounds, 5 assists, 1.6 steals, and 2.2 blocks per game (stats only achieved by Kareem Abdul-Jabbar at the time), Kevin dominated the courts and took the opportunity to end the losing streak. Facing the Nuggets and a very young Carmelo Anthony, Garnett carried Minnesota to the conference semifinals, winning the series four games to one with an average of over 25 points and nearly 15 rebounds to boot. The adventure ended in the conference finals against the Lakers. It was his last playoff campaign with the Wolves and the beginning of a significant decline for the franchise.

This victorious epic was especially important for Garnett as it finally allowed him to pay tribute to the memory of his friend and mentor Malik Sealy, who died on May 20, 2000, when his car was hit by a drunk driver. Sealy was on his way home from Garnett's

DID YOU KNOW?

While salaries in the league have skyrocketed in recent years, this was not necessarily the case in the late 1990s. At the dawn of his fourth season in the NBA, Garnett signed a contract that would make him the highest-paid player in the league between 2000 and 2004! The six-year, $126 million contract was unprecedented. KG earned more than $20 million a year for three seasons. These figures are commonplace today, but they were quite impressive at the time.

24th birthday celebration. The number 2 Garnett wore on his jersey during his time with the Nets between 2013 and 2015 was also a tribute to Sealy.

A CHANGE OF SCENERY FOR A ROSY OUTLOOK ON LIFE

Kevin Garnett arrived in Boston, MA, in the summer of 2008, in a transfer of colossal proportions – he was traded for five players and two first-round draft picks – and saw his career take a 180-degree turn.

In one summer, the Boston Celtics went from a 24-win team in 2006–2007 to the title in 2007–2008. And "Da Kid" certainly had a hand in it. Dominant even at 32, he shared the workload with Ray Allen and Paul Pierce, and the Celtics reached the NBA Finals for the first time since 1987! Garnett was his team's best player in the first rounds against the Hawks, Cavaliers, and Pistons. The Celtics went on to crush Kobe Bryant's Lakers in the finals, and the team set a new milestone by winning their first title since 1986 – an eternity for one of the league's most legendary franchises.

Kevin Garnett, meanwhile, was finally no longer a loser. In one year in Boston, he achieved what he had failed to achieve in 12 years with his longtime franchise, symbolizing the beauty and cruelty of the NBA in a single player. Coincidentally, it was the first time in 10 years that he finished a regular season with a sub-20-point average. The following years were less impressive from an individual standpoint, but Boston once again dominated the Eastern Conference and faced Los Angeles in the 2010 Finals. It was a knife-edge duel that the Lakers won in Game 7, but Garnett gave Kobe Bryant and Pau Gasol a run for their money. In six seasons, Garnett did enough to see his jersey raised to the rafters of TD Garden and his number 5 retired in Boston.

The end was unexpected, with a high-profile trade to the Nets alongside Paul Pierce that was ultimately forgettable. But as if by chance, Kevin Garnett still finished his career in Minnesota, with two seasons as a veteran with the Wolves, in a role that was more of a mentor than anything else.

A UNIQUE MENTALITY AND ENERGY

It was never a good idea to share a court with Kevin Garnett. At least not when you were playing against him. A real spark plug, an ultra-vocal leader, and

Kevin Garnett (21) looks for a pass on December 7, 2015, at the Target Center in Minneapolis.

ON THIS DAY . . .

MAY 19, 2004

In the spring of 2004, the Wolves had a unique opportunity to reach the conference finals for the first time in their history. On May 19, Kevin Garnett played in a decisive Game 7 against Chris Webber and Peja Stojaković's Sacramento Kings. The reigning MVP, the Big Ticket decided to put in one of the best performances of his career on his birthday! With 32 points, 21 rebounds, 5 blocks, and 4 steals, he played a perfect game, and Minnesota advanced to the conference finals.

a provocative genius, "KG" never gave up on the court. He knew all about intensity! Although he competed indirectly for the power forward role with Tim Duncan, who was much more focused on fundamentals and therefore less "flashy" to watch, Garnett stood out from the San Antonio player's Olympian calm. His energy helped him win four consecutive NBA rebounding titles between 2004 and 2007, making him the ninth best rebounder in league history. With the ball in his hands, he collected poster dunks and got the crowds on their feet as much as he got them making noise. Not content with winning a ring in 2008, he also took home the Defensive Player of the Year award that same year. Relieved of offensive responsibilities with Pierce and Allen at his side, he dominated everyone on the other side of the court.

Garnett missed the more physical style of the old NBA, where defenders had more freedom to make life miserable for their opponents. He liked to remind current players that they would have had a much harder time of it in the 1990s or early 2000s, before the offensive frenzy that the league is experiencing today. Just as he liked to point out that the tendency to rest stars when there are lots of games in the regular season is complete nonsense, as in his opinion players are paid to play – plain and simple. Everywhere at once, under the basket or on the perimeter, he sums up his all-round profile perfectly: "It's true that I can play anywhere, but where I'm most effective is between positions 3 and 4. Who knows, maybe I've created a new position?"

SPAIN

Pau

GASOL

BORN ON: 6 July 1980

IN: Barcelona

HEIGHT: 7'0" (2.13 m)

POSITION: Power forward/Center

PROFESSIONAL CAREER: FC Barcelona; Memphis Grizzlies; Los Angeles Lakers; Chicago Bulls; San Antonio Spurs; Milwaukee Bucks; FC Barcelona

ACHIEVEMENTS: 1 World Championship title (2006); 3 Euro titles (2009, 2011, 2015); 2 NBA Championship titles (2009, 2010); 2 Olympic silver medals (2008, 2012); 1 Olympic bronze medal (2016); 2 Spanish Championship titles (2001, 2021); 1 NBA Citizenship Award (2012)

Pau Gasol (16) during the Chicago Bulls-Philadelphia 76ers game, March 11, 2015

The circle is complete. On June 15, 2021, 20 years after his first La Liga title, Pau Gasol was crowned Barcelona champion once again. Pau Gasol Sáez's very first match in the local top elite came in January 1999, when he played for FC Barcelona against Cáceres. A fan of the Blaugrana club, the future center initially dreamed of being a soccer player. But, at 7 feet tall, the teenager was more suited to the court.

Coming from the chic suburb of Sant Boi de Llobregat, Pau's family were competition enthusiasts, and his younger brother Marc would follow in Pau's footsteps under the hoop. After starting out at CB Cornellà, Pau completed his training at the Barça school and, at the age of 16, played with the hopefuls. The 2000–2001 season ended on a high note for Barça and its gifted player. As Spanish champion, Pau was even voted MVP at the end of the final and reveled in the double achieved at the end of the Copa del Rey final. The future belonged to him, but he faced a big upheaval during the summer. Initially on the Atlanta Hawks' radar at the time of the NBA draft, Pau Gasol finally joined the Grizzlies. Except he didn't head for Vancouver, but Memphis, where the Canadian franchise had relocated.

ON THIS DAY . . .

MARCH 7, 2007
Pau Gasol made it his motto: "All records are made to be broken." That's the rule of sport. On March 7, 2007, he became the Grizzlies' all-time leading scorer. With 7,801 points, the Catalan power forward outscored American forward Shareef Abdur-Rahim, former record-holder with the Memphis franchise. Despite his performance that evening, Pau couldn't prevent the team's defeat by the Toronto Raptors (87–94). By the time he left Memphis in early 2008, Pau had reached a total of 8,966 points with the Grizzlies.

OFF TO TENNESSEE!

An exceptional forward, Pau Gasol was an impressive shot blocker, which gave him a natural talent for rebounding. In NBA, he quickly earned the role of a go-to guy – the player who takes care of everything – with teammates less involved in making plays. In March 2006, he scored his first triple-double, with 21 points, 12 assists, and 12 rebounds in the same game. As soon as the season resumed, he missed the first 23 games due to a fractured metatarsal in his foot.

In 2008, following an agreement between the Grizzlies and the Lakers, Pau Gasol was transferred to Los Angeles. What's even funnier is that he ran into his brother Marc, who had been recruited by the Memphis franchise. The Grizzlies picked up the rights to the younger brother when the older one was transferred to California!

Now in Los Angeles, Pau's chemistry with Lakers MVP Kobe Bryant was pure magic – they could find each other on the court with their eyes closed. Gasol may have been the first Spaniard to

qualify for an NBA final, but one last doubt remained: he was criticized for lacking that killer instinct in crucial games. The following season, the Pau silenced the last skeptics. In the final against the Orlando Magic, since he wasn't the center of attention, he could relax and play without pressure, almost under the radar, and showed his enormous progress in terms of consistency.

This time, he became the first basketball player from Spain to wear the coveted ring. And, when summer came, he also became the first European to win a Euro just after winning the NBA title. On the go for months, Pau Gasol pulled off a double the following season in the NBA, but mentally exhausted, he declined his invitation to the 2010 World Cup. A year later, he returned to a major tournament, leading Spain to Euro success against the French in the final (98–85), with the dominant Catalan scoring 17 points.

Everything came to a head in the summer of 2014, with a solid-gold offer from the Bulls, but the transfer was delayed because Chicago needed to lighten its payroll! At the 2016 Rio Games, with 3,331 points, bronze medalist Pau Gasol became the all-time leading scorer for the Spanish national team. The power forward discovered a new horizon when he joined the Spurs in 2016, and hit it off with Tony Parker, who was impressed by the Spanish recruit. "Pau is exemplary in the way he takes care of his body and in his diet," said Parker. "The proof is he never has serious injuries."

THE RETURN OF THE WONDER KID TO LA RAMBLA!

After having been traded from the Spurs to the Bucks in early 2019, Pau signed with the Trail Blazers in July. But, plagued by foot and ankle injuries, Pau left Portland in November without playing a single game. Deprived of the World Cup in China in 2019, Pau Gasol took some time off to recover and, in a significant move in February 2021, he returned to Barcelona. In May 2021, the Catalan power forward even contested the EuroLeague final with his beloved club, but the Turks of Anadolu Efes were merciless (81–86). Three

Tony Parker and Pau Gasol during the France-Spain warm-up match at the Olympic Games in Paris, July 15, 2012.

DID YOU KNOW?

Due to a fracture of the navicular bone in his left foot, Pau Gasol missed the 2019 Conference Finals with the Milwaukee Bucks against Toronto. He also missed out on a reunion with his brother Marc, the Raptors' center, who won 100–94. Despite the disappointment, Pau's younger brother Marc prepared as best he could and, for the NBA Finals against the Golden State Warriors, "Marco" did not miss the opportunity to join his older brother, Pau, on the winners' podium after a 4–2 success. It was also the first time in the history of the American league that two brothers have been champions.

months later, at the Tokyo Olympics, alongside his brother Marc, the Spanish giant performed his last waltz for the national team, in the quarterfinal loss to the United States (81–95).

On October 5, 2021, at the foot of Montjuïc Hill and with a teary voice, Pau Gasol announced the end of his career. At 41 years of age, the jewel of Catalonia shed tears, between a testament and a tribute: "I wanted to give a special mention to Kobe Bryant. I would have loved so much for him to be here today, but fate decided otherwise, and it is sometimes cruel. I miss Black Mamba so much! He taught me how to become a better player, a better competitor and, above all, he made me understand what it meant to be a leader."

FRANCE

Rudy GOBERT

BORN ON: 26 June 1992

IN: Saint-Quentin

HEIGHT: 7'1" (2.16 m)

POSITION: Center

PROFESSIONAL CAREER: Cholet Basket; Utah Jazz; Bakersfield Jam; Utah Jazz; Minnesota Timberwolves

ACHIEVEMENTS: 2 Olympic silver medals (2020, 2024); 2 bronze medals at the World Championships (2014, 2019); 1 silver medal at EuroBasket (2022); 1 bronze medal at EuroBasket (2015)

Rudy Gobert (15) during the Nancy-Cholet match during the 2012 Semaine des As (Leaders Cup) at Roanne's Halle André Vacheresse on February 17, 2012.

Knocked out right from the start. On April 15, 2017, for his very first playoff appearance, Rudy Gobert's performance lasted just 13 short seconds. While he was managing a screen to protect his partner Gordon Hayward, the French center made contact with the Los Angeles Clippers' forward Luc Mbah, and his left knee gave way. A cruel verdict, as it was indeed a sprain that ended Rudy's dreams of glory.

A few weeks earlier, everything was going well with "Gobzilla" (a reference to the gigantic Japanese monster). The man who has also been dubbed "the French Rejection" for his ability to block any opponent with his sprawling arms, had just extended his contract with the Utah Jazz for $100 million over four years. In 15 years, the kid from Saint-Quentin had gone from his native France to Salt Lake City with astonishing ease.

Although it all began in the boxing ring, Rudy Gobert quickly abandoned the gloves after a childhood prank. In the time it took to trip over a plastic shark lying on the floor and land on an extremely sharp box cutter, the young man ended up in the emergency room with eight stitches in his hand. Goodbye to the noble art. After his hand healed, Rudy finally turned to basketball to satisfy his hyperactivity.

ON THIS DAY . . .

MARCH 25, 2019

On the Vivint Arena court, on March 25, 2019, Rudy Gobert entered NBA legend by breaking the record for dunks in a season. On this victory night over the Phoenix Suns (125–192), the French center also broke the record that Dwight Howard, with the Orlando Magic, had held since the 2007–2008 season, by blocking the opposing hoop 270 times. A record achieved in 74 matches. His reaction on Twitter: "Just a kid from Saint-Quentin." Despite his soaring ambitions, it was a way to keep his feet on the ground and stay proud of his roots.

THE BIG LEAP TO THE PROS

On the verge of turning 18, Rudy joined Cholet's training center, where, in addition to his exploits under the hoop, he earned a scientific baccalaureate. On February 10, 2011, Gobert made his debut with Cholet during the Semaine des As, replacing the injured American Randal Falker. And, despite the defeat to the formidable Pau-Orthez team (76–78), the young center's career was launched.

Then came the incredible episode of his 2013 draft candidacy. Rudy was first chosen by the Denver Nuggets, before being immediately traded to the Utah Jazz. This didn't upset him too much. "Ever since I was little, I never set limits for myself," he recalled. "I've always aimed very high." This impression was confirmed as soon as he took his first steps on the NBA courts. Tyrone Corbin, his Jazz coach, gave him regular playing time and, in the 2014–2015 season, he achieved his first double-double.

NOT SINCE TONY PARKER IN 2003 . . .

Gobzilla became the first Frenchman to take part in the Rising Stars Challenge, which pits a selection made in the USA against the rest of the world. With Giannis Antetokounmpo, Andrew Wiggins, and Bojan Bogdanović alongside him, Rudy Gobert scored 18 points, grabbed 12 rebounds, and made 3 blocks. The jersey-clad expatriates pulled off the feat of beating the best of the best (121–112) at the Barclays Center in Brooklyn. Rudy's arm span discouraged his opponents from attempting any dunks or lay-ups. By protecting the hoop, Gobert has become a renowned rim-protector on US courts. A real rebound vacuum cleaner, he leaves nothing but crumbs for even the most seasoned competitors and is considered one of the best inside defenders in the league.

Rudy Gobert (27), member of the French team, during the men's gold medal match, on the 15th day of the Tokyo Olympic Games, at the Saitama Super Arena, on August 7, 2021.

His behind-the-scenes work isn't always recognized for what it's worth by those obsessed with statistical overkill. Behind the avalanche of numbers and analytical tables, Rudy is rarely glorified. "My offensive qualities are regularly underestimated," he said, "because they don't often show up on paper." This excellent screen player's style benefits first and foremost his teammates. We can always quibble about his game, which is considered limited outside the court – he rarely makes three-pointers – or about his more neutral performances in the playoffs, but nothing can shake the Saint-Quentin giant.

In the 2018–2019 season, paired with Derrick Favors, Rudy demanded a greater role on offense, just to silence a few bitter critics. A few months later, with 47 consecutive games and an

Los Angeles Lakers' Carmelo Anthony (7) attempts to block the dunk of Utah Jazz's Rudy Gobert (27) during a game at Vivint Arena in Salt Lake City, March 31, 2022.

DID YOU KNOW?

The French center did not choose number 27 at random. Drafted in 27th position in 2013, Rudy was frustrated at being so low down and decided to take fate into his own hands. Farewelling the number 15 of his debut, Rudy adopted 27 and decided to make it his lucky number. He wears it today both at club level and with the French national team. The number has finally become a lucky charm not only on the court, but also in his everyday life!

average of over 50 percent shooting success, Rudy was racking up the stats better than anyone in the last 30 years in the NBA. Beyond the stats, it's the tribute from his teammate Joe Ingles that best captures the man's qualities: "I wouldn't be the defender I am if Rudy wasn't there. I wouldn't press opponents so hard if I wasn't aware that he's behind me protecting the circle." That's all, folks!

A four-time Defensive Player of the Year, Gobert remains one of the best defensive centers in the NBA. His contract extension in October 2024 solidified his position as a key element of the Wolves' collective.

UNITED STATES

Allen IVERSON

BORN ON: 7 June 1975

IN: Hampton, Virginia

HEIGHT: 6'0" (1.83 m)

POSITION: Guard

PROFESSIONAL CAREER: Philadelphia 76ers; Denver Nuggets; Detroit Pistons; Memphis Grizzlies; Philadelphia 76ers; Beşiktaş JK

ACHIEVEMENTS: 1 NBA regular season MVP title (2001); 1 Olympic bronze medal (2004)

Denver Nuggets' Allen Iverson (3) drives by in the game against the Minnesota Timberwolves on January 4, 2008. The Denver Nuggets won 118–107.

Although he never won a championship, Allen Iverson is considered one of the best guards in history, playing in a position that has been graced by the likes of Michael Jordan and Kobe Bryant. He left his mark during his 14-season NBA career. Relatively short (6'0") in a league where the average height is close to 6 foot 6 (2 m), he was an inspiration to many "small" players. The smallest and lightest MVP in history, Allen was inducted into the Hall of Fame in his first year of eligibility in 2016. Iverson revolutionized the game with his crossovers and scoring but also shook up the NBA with his style on and off the court. With historic scoring averages, he ranks seventh in career scoring in the league and third in the playoffs. He was named the league's leading scorer four times, making him one of the best offensive players in history.

DID YOU KNOW?

While Iverson spent his professional career on the NBA courts, he could just as easily have devoted it to the fields of the NFL. A true quarterback phenomenon during his high school years, Allen stood out for his ability to play multiple positions, on offense, defense, and even on special teams. He did all this while racking up impressive statistics and playing basketball on the side. Courted by some of the best programs in the country, including those that lead straight to the NFL, he was caught up in legal problems that ended his dreams of playing football, before Georgetown rekindled his passion for basketball.

CULTURAL ICON

Allen Iverson represents a style, a way of life, and a hip-hop culture that he instilled in the NBA. A "product of the street," he burst onto the NBA scene wearing baggy pants, diamond chains, and more tattoos than was typical for the time. His cornrows stood out, and on the court, he didn't think twice about wearing a headband or, later, after an arm injury, playing with a sleeve. Popularized by his sponsor Reebok, the slogan "I am what I am" perfectly describes the man whose style choices would eventually prompt NBA boss David Stern to introduce a dress code in 2005 for all players. They were required to attend games dressed in "business casual" – something close to a suit. In fact, the phenomenon was all-encompassing and reached across the entire league – an influence he still claims today.

With "the Answer," hip-hop finally arrived in the NBA, although it was already a big part of basketball. Iverson explained this several times after his career: "When I played basketball, when I went to the park, I didn't go in a suit. I'm going to play basketball. I go there with the clothes I'm going to wear and the clothes the guys in my neighborhood wear. For me, suits have always been clothes you wear to funerals."

Spectacular as anything, Allen didn't care too much about his shooting percentages or turnovers, and luckily, neither did his fans. While he may have skipped practice or sometimes got into heated arguments with his coach, Allen accomplished feats never before seen on the courts. His crossovers were unprecedented, and he magnified the art of dribbling, enough to leave a certain Michael Jordan in the dust twice in the same play. His shots came at the end of unlikely plays, which made him even harder to defend. Indeed, who could read his moves, anticipate his shots or dribbles, or guess what was going through his mind? The perfect player for the All-Star Game, Allen Iverson won two MVP awards and was selected 11 times, adding to his already impressive list of personal awards. Awards which he collected at the very beginning of the century . . .

THE YEAR 2001: ONE TO REMEMBER

The 76ers reached the finals after a playoff campaign in which Iverson averaged just over 32 points per game, in a series against the Bucks, Raptors, and Pacers, all of whom fell to the guard. However, once qualified, the Sixers faced the team to beat at the start of the 21st century: the Lakers, who were undefeated in the playoffs and defending champions. The first game was tight, going into overtime, with Iverson scoring 48 points. But just as the Lakers were leading by three points and the opportunity seemed to have disappeared, the MVP rallied and scored five straight points to give his team the lead.

That's when, with around 50 seconds left, Iverson found himself one-on-one against a certain Tyronn Lue. Shaken by Allen's crossover, poor Tyronn Lue tripped

ON THIS DAY . . .

NOVEMBER 16, 2010

Arriving at Beşiktaş in the fall of 2010, Allen Iverson was the greatest American player to have ever stepped onto a European court during his career. However, although he thrilled basketball fans with his debut on November 16, 2010, his performances were inconsistent, and he was forced to return to the United States after a calf injury cut his adventure short. His 11 short games are not particularly memorable (averaging 11.5 points in the Euro Cup and 14.3 in the Turkish league), at least not more than the rumors that he simply needed to replenish his bank account with a nice check, as he was suspected of being broke at the time.

and crashed to the floor, tangled in his tormentor's feet. On the ground, with his butt flat on the floor, he watched as the star casually stepped over him like he was nothing more than a bump in the road. The image went viral in the basketball world and is now considered one of the greatest examples of trash talking of all time – without a word even being spoken. Philadelphia went on to win the game and knock Los Angeles out of the playoffs for the first time.

Allen Iverson (3) shows his style on the court on March 20, 2000.

Much to Iverson's regret, his trophy cabinet would never be adorned with the major league's most prestigious award, as he would never reach the finals again. He only won one of the six postseason series he subsequently participated in. He even declared one day that he had spent his entire life chasing a ring and never won it; even though he never chased the title of top scorer, he nevertheless won four times.

ALLEN, THE DARK SIDE

Unfortunately, Allen Iverson's character cannot be summed up by his on-court achievements and his cultural influence. Born in a ghetto in Hampton, Virginia, Iverson grew up in poverty, surrounded by violence, drugs, and bad company. This environment contributed greatly to tarnishing his image and sometimes jeopardizing his career.

It all began even before he reached adulthood and well before the NBA. In 1993, he was arrested and sentenced to 15 years in prison, 10 of which were suspended, for allegedly taking part in a bowling alley brawl that got completely out of hand. Although the governor of Virginia granted Allen clemency after four months in prison (and the conviction was overturned in 1995), he had to give up on his football dreams (see "Did you know?" section on p. 85). And while Georgetown was eventually persuaded to recruit the player, who was still playing point guard at the time, it could all have come crashing down much earlier.

LeBron JAMES

BORN ON: 30 December 1984

IN: Akron, Ohio

HEIGHT: 6'9" (2.06 m)

POSITION: Forward

PROFESSIONAL CAREER: Cleveland Cavaliers; Miami Heat; Cleveland Cavaliers; Los Angeles Lakers

ACHIEVEMENTS: 3 Olympic gold medals (2008, 2012, 2024); 4 NBA championship titles (2012, 2013, 2016, 2020); 4 NBA regular season MVP titles (2009, 2010, 2012, 2013); 4 NBA Finals MVP titles (2012, 2013, 2016, 2020)

LeBron James celebrates victory at the 2020 NBA All-Star Game at Chicago's United Center, February 16, 2020.

A snake surrounded by roses and adorned with the numbers 8 and 24 and the slogan "Mamba 4 life" all tattooed on the thigh, engraved on his skin. All in tribute to his lifelong rival and unforgettable friend Kobe Bryant, who died in a helicopter accident in January 2020. It was a tragedy that left its mark on the entire US basketball community, and particularly on LeBron James, who was affected like never before. Although "the King" has weathered many storms, this one was so sudden and so cruel that the Akron giant felt his throne wobble.

A few days after the tragedy, in a cruel twist of fate, LBJ broke the NBA scoring record of the Lakers' Black Mamba, with a staggering 33,643 points in 17 seasons. LeBron James is no stranger to pulling off individual feats. Between his early success at the highest level and longevity, he has always pushed the boundaries. In addition to his record 16 All-Star Game appearances, LeBron has also become the third most prolific scorer in the NBA, behind the legendary Kareem Abdul-Jabbar and Karl Malone.

ON THIS DAY . . .

MARCH 12, 2022
For the 15th time in his career, LeBron James ended a match with 50 points or more. A feat achieved on March 12, 2022, against the Washington Wizards (122–109). Another remarkable fact: in less than a week, LBJ was a repeat offender, since six days earlier, against the Golden State Warriors, he had crushed the team's defense (scoring 56 points). You have to go back to Kobe Bryant's 2006–2007 season to find any trace of a Lakers player with over 100 points in two games.

THE CHOSEN ONE

Before basketball, LeBron was seriously considering football. His mother Gloria didn't want to see her son hanging around the neighborhood, so she pushed him into sport. His skill under the basket was confirmed on the Northeast Ohio Shooting Stars. He would then play on the varsity team at St. Vincent–St. Mary High School.

As a student, LBJ hid his first tattoos with bandages so as not to violate his school's rules banning them. Very early on, experts saw him as the worthy heir of a certain Michael Jordan and immediately christened him "the Chosen One."

James was drafted by his hometown team, the Cleveland Cavaliers, as the first overall pick in 2003. In his first season with the Cavaliers, LeBron became the youngest player in NBA history, at 20 years and 183 days, to score over 2,000 points. He was also named Rookie of the Year. In February 2006, nothing fazed him, and he became the youngest basketball player to win the title of best player at the All-Star Game in Houston. LeBron James was also smashing every record. *Forbes* magazine ranked him

LeBron James (6) of the Los Angeles Lakers about to score during the game against the Houston Rockets at the Toyota Center in Houston, March 9, 2022

as the richest person under 25, with an estimated annual income of $27 million!

In July 2010, the first cracks appeared in the idol's previously flawless image, which triggered real resentment when he announced his departure for Miami. Criticism rained down: some observers considered him to be a megalomaniac, while others saw him as a "wimp" who never stood up for his teammates in a fight. On the sporting front, some commentators unfairly found his three-point shooting statistics low.

AT THE TOP OF HIS GAME

It's the ultimate achievement for this force of nature, who possesses a level of athleticism that is rarely equaled. His body type is almost perfect for a modern forward. It's a treat to follow him with his back to the basket, then watch him turn around to score a perfect shot. In the team, no one regrets the altruistic side of the champion, who specializes in surgical passes. Ambidextrous, LeBron James signs his contracts with his left hand but aims for the basket with his right. So, whatever criticisms may be heaped on his career here and there, there's no stopping this natural leader.

For his debut with the Heat, his involvement was notable but short-lived. He won his first NBA title with Miami in

DID YOU KNOW?

With a keen business sense, LeBron James knows how to make his immeasurable fortune grow. Guided by his right-hand man and childhood friend Maverick Carter, in 2011 the King even became a shareholder in Liverpool Football Club! The NBA star ended up with a 2 percent stake in the English club after a cross deal with his company LRMR and his partner Fenway Sports Group, who bought the Reds. As for the fans, they recently enjoyed LBJ's visit to Anfield, celebrated with the traditional "You'll Never Walk Alone."

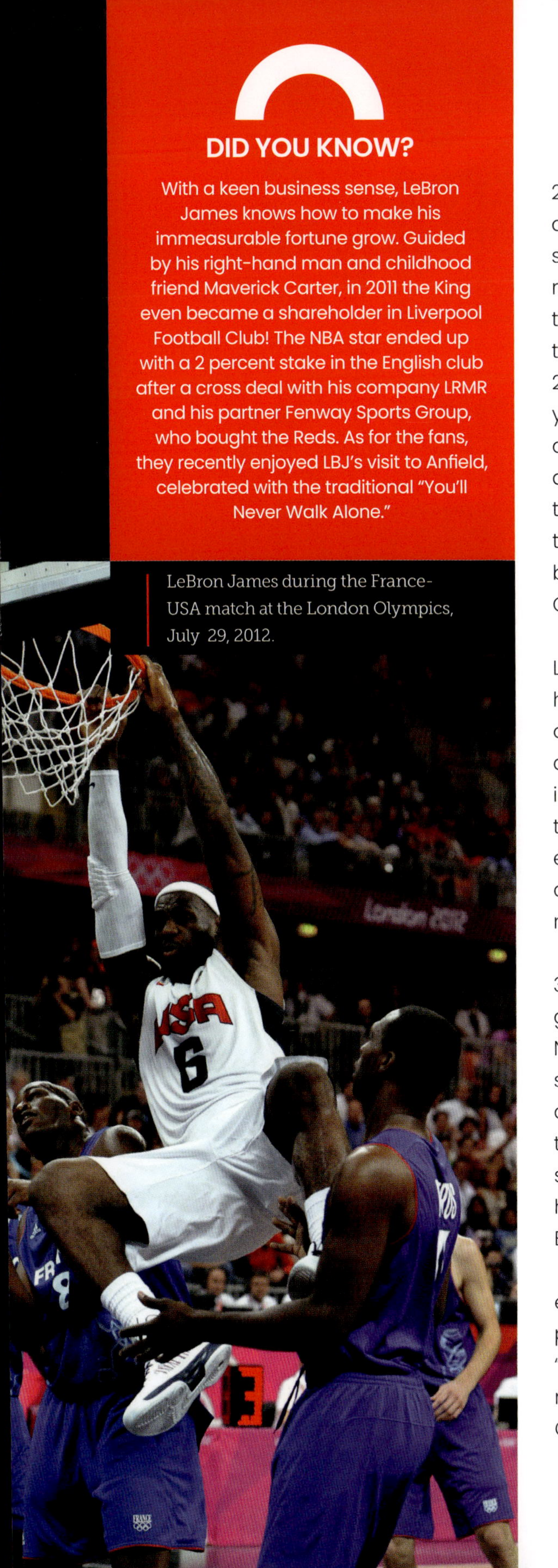

LeBron James during the France-USA match at the London Olympics, July 29, 2012.

2012 and the second the year after, being declared MVP on both occasions. Two seasons later, he made a media-hyped return to Cleveland. "A heart choice," said the rarely satisfied LeBron James. With the Cavs, he won the NBA title again in 2016. In February 2018, LBJ became the youngest player to exceed 30,000 points, all complemented by 8,000 rebounds and 8,000 assists. Then, two years later, the icon won his fourth title, this time with the Lakers, and became one of the few basketball players to have won the Holy Grail with three different franchises.

Remaining true to his roots, LeBron opened a nursery school in his hometown of Akron and created an association to combat school absenteeism. His dedication to activism is such that he isn't afraid to stand up to Donald Trump. The king of the courts even helped found the More than a Vote association, which fights for the voting rights of African Americans.

On December 20, 2021, at nearly 37 years of age, James defied time. The good LeBron had spent half his life in the NBA, with as many days accumulated since his draft in 2003 as since his birth – a mind-boggling total of 6,752 days with the NBA. If he has managed to maintain such a consistent level under the basket, he owes it largely to his partner, Savannah Brinson, whom he met in high school.

"She has always been by my side, even when there were no cameras or photographers," said LeBron James. "I wouldn't be here if she hadn't supported me." Perhaps that is the secret of the Chosen One's success.

UNITED STATES

Earvin "Magic" JOHNSON

BORN ON: 14 August 1959

IN: Lansing, Michigan

HEIGHT: 6'9" (2.06 m)

POSITION: Point guard

PROFESSIONAL CAREER: Los Angeles Lakers

ACHIEVEMENTS: 1 Olympic gold medal (1992); 5 NBA championship titles (1980, 1982, 1985, 1987, 1988); 3 regular season MVP titles (1987, 1989, 1990); 3 MVP titles in the NBA Finals (1980, 1982, 1987); 1 NBA Citizenship Award (1992)

Earvin "Magic" Johnson in action during the Angola-USA match at the Barcelona Olympic Games, July 30, 1992.

The fact is, in the Johnson family, basketball runs in the veins. Earvin Senior was a high school basketball player, and his half-brother Michael was also very good. The orange ball was like oxygen for young Earvin Junior, already a grown-up in a family where he took on the responsibility of raising his half-brother and two half-sisters.

Like doing piano scales, the young man was constantly practicing dribbling and attempting lay-ups with both hands. At the club, his coach advised him to shoot with his weak arm, just to make things a little less easy for the teenager – that's how comfortable he was around the paint. Attending the majority-white Everett High School, the gifted player joined the basketball team, where he was initially rejected by his teammates. But through his talent and character, young Johnson took his team from an average level to a formidable and feared team. The local press was amazed and quickly dubbed him "Magic," a nickname that would follow him throughout his career. When he came of age, the ball wizard joined the Michigan State Spartans and then, in 1978, he tried his luck at the draft for the first time.

It turned out to be a complete flop. His performance was close to zero and Kansas City turned him down. The following season, Earvin "Magic" Johnson got his revenge and agreed to a deal with the Lakers for $500,000 a year. Not bad for a rookie!

From his very first NBA appearances, his bond with the legendary Kareem Abdul-Jabbar was obvious. A few months later, he experienced his first All-Star Game with Larry Bird, another rookie who would also make a name for himself. King of the famous no-look pass, Johnson demonstrated incredible dexterity in his fluid and efficient movements. As a natural fighter with unfailing charisma, he was always capable of a flash of genius. The versatility of this chameleon in the paint was a coach's dream. The only downside – Magic Johnson wasn't much of a scorer, even if his triple-double record would make some people swoon.

DID YOU KNOW?

A fan of the French Riviera, Magic Johnson often goes there on vacation and supports AS Monaco and its Roca Team. With the American team, he has fond memories of the preparation phase on the Rock of Monaco before the Barcelona Olympics. The French team even served as sparring partners at the Stade Louis-II in July 1992, a few days before the opening of the Olympic tournament. Charles Barkley, Larry Bird, Michael Jordan, and Magic Johnson easily defeated Jim Bilba's Blues (111–71).

THE FIRST TIME AROUND

In his first season at the highest level, Magic clinched his first NBA title in a tough fight, evolving from a hopeful talent into a resilient leader.

Against the Philadelphia 76ers in the final, Kareem Abdul-Jabbar was injured during the fifth game and his young teammate had to replace him as center. Earvin gave a breathtaking performance in the sixth game in an unfamiliar position, scoring 42 points in a row. He became the first rookie to be voted best player of the final!

Before the second title in 1982, Lakers owner Jerry Buss announced that Magic Johnson was a player "for 25 years and $25 million," an astronomical contract for the time. The slogan made Californian fans go crazy. Behind the scenes, however, the situation was far from idyllic. There were hints of friction between Johnson and his coach, Paul Westhead, whose predictable tactics irritated the big-hearted point guard.

Publicly, the two men no longer hid their disagreement, but the atmosphere became unbearable. Westhead was fired, and some of the faithful put the blame on Magic who, for some fans, had behaved like a diva.

With the arrival of a new coach, Pat Riley, Earvin felt liberated and put in a string of stellar performances.

Earvin "Magic" Johnson (32) at the Los Angeles Lakers-Houston Rockets NBA game in Houston, February 24, 1996.

Earvin "Magic" Johnson celebrates his gold medal, following the Dream Team's final victory over Croatia at the Barcelona Olympic Games, August 8, 1992

ON THIS DAY . . .

AUGUST 8, 1992

At Barcelona's Palau dels Esports, on August 8, 1992, the United States had just crushed Croatia in the Olympic final (117–85). At the award ceremony, Magic Johnson almost missed out on a place on the podium. Out of loyalty to his sponsor, Nike, he refused to be seen with the competitor who dressed the Dream Team. It took the intervention of Phil Knight, Nike's CEO, who was present at the event, to restore order. A compromise was reached, and the US point guard carried the American flag on his shoulders to hide the logo that caused the dispute.

After suffering a knee injury during the 1985–1986 season, Magic came back stronger and was selected to play in the All-Star Game, becoming the first player in history to receive over a million votes in his favor. The Lakers went on to win back-to-back championships in 1987 and 1988, unseen since the Boston Celtics in 1968–1969.

THE SHOCK OF NOVEMBER 7, 1991

This was the day that Magic Johnson officially announced he had been diagnosed HIV-positive, but that he was continuing his career on the courts. He was selected for the Dream Team, which went on to dominate the Barcelona Olympic Games, scoring more than 100 points per game.

The illness, the misconceptions it carried, and an exhausting course of antiretroviral drugs squeezed the end of Magic Johnson's career. Like a crooner on the comeback trail, he gave a false farewell, before making an unremarkable comeback in 1996.

Twenty years later, he was appointed president of the Lakers, but the experience was cut short. After weeks of conflict with Lakers' general manager Rob Pelinka, Johnson suddenly called it quits in April 2019. Despite his involvement in recruiting LeBron James, he was clear in his choice: "When it's no longer fun for me, when I think I no longer have the power to make decisions, then I have to leave." Still, for Magic Johnson, everything ends with a big smile, the corner of his lips curling up.

UNITED STATES

Michael

JORDAN

BORN ON: 17 February 1963

IN: Brooklyn, New York

HEIGHT: 6′6″ (1.98 m)

POSITION: Guard

PROFESSIONAL CAREER: Chicago Bulls; Washington Wizards

ACHIEVEMENTS: 2 Olympic gold medals (1984, 1992); 6 NBA champion titles (1991, 1992, 1993, 1996, 1997, 1998); 5 NBA regular season MVP titles (1988, 1991, 1992, 1996, 1998); 6 NBA Finals MVP titles (1991, 1992, 1993, 1996, 1997, 1998)

Michael Jordan at a game at Chicago's United Center, December 11, 1997

The standing ovation lasted over three minutes. On April 16, 2003, 20,000 spectators at the First Union Center were gripped with emotion, as a legend prepared for his final act – right in the heart of rival territory. Wearing his Washington Wizards jersey, Michael Jordan played his final seconds on an NBA court. To honor the hero, at the request of his coach Larry Brown, the Sixers' point guard Eric Snow knowingly fouled MJ, to give him two final free throws.

Further proof that the retirement of this absolute legend at the age of 40, after more than 1,000 NBA games, made a lasting impression, the Miami Heat immediately made a bold decision. Although Michael Jordan had never played there, the Florida club decided to remove the star's lucky number 23 from its squad! Under the American flag, Jordan's star shines forever.

DID YOU KNOW?

A true star, Michael Jordan has regularly appeared in various films and TV series over the past 20 years, playing himself. In 1996, he starred in the feature film *Space Jam*. Film buffs also discovered him in Spike Lee's *He Got Game*. The legendary basketball player also appeared in season 5 of *My Wife and Kids*, as well as in the documentary-miniseries *The Last Dance*.

A STAR IS BORN

When the rookie arrived at Chicago's O'Hare airport in September 1984, having just transferred from the University of North Carolina, the future was his. However, no one came to roll out the red carpet for him. In total anonymity, the young New Yorker was left to his own devices. His new franchise, the Bulls, didn't even bother to pick him up at the terminal exit. A limousine driver, George Koehler, suggested that Jordan climb aboard his shiny car for a tour of the Windy City. For the modest sum of $25, "Mike" accepted. A sincere and lasting friendship was born.

From his first performances with the Bulls, Michael, with his hardened steel mentality, amazed with his explosiveness. *Sports Illustrated* had the foresight to feature him on the cover with the headline: "A star is born." Watching him inside a sports complex that sometimes seemed too small for him, basketball experts were mesmerized. Each bound of the genius, each jump-shot amazed the crowds. His nickname, "Air Jordan," was by no means a misnomer, and he made it his trademark. Thanks to his extraordinary core strength, he was also declared "Mr. Hang Time," for his natural ability to remain suspended high above the rim for longer than any other player. His iconic dunk from the free-throw line left even the toughest critics stunned. With incredible ease and dominant in defensive tasks, Michael Jordan also had the luxury of being effective in clutch time.

It's hard not to be won over by this 24-carat diamond who, throughout his career, never lost a single NBA final. All the records, all the statistics were challenged by an intergalactic Michael Jordan. As for anecdotes, they abound on the courts. Every move the champion made was analyzed. His habit of sticking out his tongue when he took a free throw was put under the shrink's microscope. The experts were convinced: "His Majesty Jordan uses this habit to better tune out his surroundings and improve his concentration."

At the same time, his selfishness annoyed some people. Rare critics have denounced his manipulative and resentful side. Michael Jordan dribbles on without missing a beat: "Some people have called me a bully. But they never won anything! I always wanted to win, but I wanted to bring my teammates with me. That was my mentality." After all, isn't an oversized ego the hallmark of world sports stars? In 1991, during a match against the Denver Nuggets, young center Dikembe Mutombo tried to take a swipe at the legend. Michael Jordan responded in the best possible way, scoring 37 points that day and converting two free throws – with his eyes closed!

HE'S BACK!

After nine seasons of success and glory with the Chicago Bulls, in October 1993, His Airness announced his decision to retire from basketball. A dramatic event had brought Jordan's rise to an abrupt halt – his father James was murdered in a North Carolina parking lot by two teenagers. After a period of mourning, Michael Jordan made a comeback in baseball and joined the Birmingham Barons as an outfielder.

And then, in March 1995, a joyful announcement, slamming home like a dunk – "I'm back!" – sent the media

Michael Jordan of the Chicago Bulls during the second match of the 1998 NBA Finals against the Utah Jazz at the Delta Center in Salt Lake City, June 5, 1998.

ON THIS DAY . . .

NOVEMBER 23, 2016

On November 23, 2016, in Washington, DC, Barack Obama presented the Presidential Medal of Freedom to Michael Jordan. During the president's speech, the Bulls' legendary guard couldn't hold back his tears. "He's more than just the best player," said Barack Obama, proud and happy to honor such a sporting legend.

Michael Jordan (23) of the Chicago Bulls during an NBA game against the Miami Heat on January 1, 1996.

Michael Jordan, member of the US national basketball team, on the court at the 1992 Barcelona Olympics.

into a frenzy. His Airness was back under the hoops. Millions of feverish television viewers followed his return against the Indiana Pacers. It was a shock result on the small screen – 55 points for the Genius.

Michael Jordan made a second comeback in 2001 with the Washington Wizards. In the midst of a troubled period for his country, he donated his salary to the families of the victims of 9/11. A motorbike and golf enthusiast and restaurant owner, the all-time legend continued to rake in the greenbacks once he put away his sneakers. Even in retirement, MJ reportedly earns over $30,000 an hour from his investments. The eternal basketball fan, he took on a new challenge in March 2010 when he bought the Charlotte Hornets franchise, formerly known as the Bobcats. A return to his roots in North Carolina, where it all began.

Toni
KUKOČ

BORN ON: 18 September 1968

IN: Split

HEIGHT: 6′11″ (2.11 m)

POSITION: Power forward

PROFESSIONAL CAREER: Jugoplastika Split; Benetton Treviso; Chicago Bulls; Philadelphia 76ers; Atlanta Hawks; Milwaukee Bucks

ACHIEVEMENTS: 1 World Championship title (1990); 2 Euro titles (1989, 1991); 3 NBA Championship titles (1996, 1997, 1998); 3 European Championship titles (1989, 1990, 1991); 2 silver Olympic medals (1988, 1992)

Toni Kukoč (7) attempts to score a basket against Dale Davis (32) of the Indiana Pacers during Game 7 of the Eastern Conference Finals at the United Center in Chicago, May 31, 1998.

By declaring that "one basket makes a man happy, while one assist makes two," Toni Kukoč created his trademark motto. Admittedly, "the Croatian Sensation" was full of energy and audacity, and could have taken all the credit, but teamwork has always been his credo. With a disconcerting ease in the technical domain, Toni was a force to be reckoned with in everything he did on the court. And when it came to passes, he was a treat – blindly, behind the back, or even behind the head, no move was too wild for him.

Endowed with an above-average strength of character, Toni must have shown a lot of resilience when he took his first steps in the NBA, because he received a lukewarm welcome. What's more, he had to silence the US media skeptics. Yet from a very young age, Toni Kukoč was admired by his coaches.

ON THIS DAY . . .

AUGUST 1, 1987
With the young Yugoslavians at the World Youth Championship on August 1, 1987, Toni Kukoč, with incredible maturity, managed 11 three-point shots out of 12 attempted against the American college players. They were sent back to the classroom at the end of the final (86–76). With 37 points in total, the Split forward was unstoppable. "Since that day, I've never managed to get anywhere near those kinds of statistics. During the match, everything fell into place!" Toni still marvels about it to this day.

TABLE TENNIS, HIS FIRST LOVE

Toni's father Ante was a goalkeeper for Hajduk Split, a club that ran in his blood. Then, as a teenager Toni became an excellent table tennis player, covering his bedroom walls with his medals in this sport.

In fact, Kukoč only discovered basketball at the age of 14. A coach spotted the tall beanpole among his friends, towering over them as the group enjoyed themselves on a beach. From his first selections in the youth categories, he didn't waste any time. Victory at the Europe Under-16 Championship in 1985 was followed two years later by a truly impressive display with another title at the World Youth Championship in Italy. As soon as Toni started with Jugoplastika within the elite, he won the Yugoslavian Grail in 1988. The team went on to defy all odds at the end of the 1989 season. During the European Final Four, the gifted team from Split surprised Barça in the semifinals (87–77), with Toni scoring 24 points!

The Croatians confirmed their status with a crowning glory against Maccabi Tel Aviv (75–69). It wasn't a one-off victory, as Jugoplastika reigned over the continent for the next two seasons. After the victorious Euro 1989, with an unstoppable Kukoč named MVP, the Yugoslavians won the absolute crown at the World Cup, having dethroned the USA and the USSR! On the home front, Jugoplastika achieved the double in 1991, beating arch-rivals Partizan Belgrade. Despite the blow, the Belgrade fans rose to give a standing ovation to Toni Kukoč. This shows the deep respect the Serbian public had for him at a time when Yugoslavia, as a nation, was in the process of breaking up.

AT THE GIANTS' TABLE

Having just transferred to Treviso, Italy, Toni won the Italian title. He dreamed of a fourth C1 crown when the Final Four came to Piraeus, Athens, in 1993. But in the final, the French team Limoges CSP, coached by Toni's former mentor Božidar Maljković, beat Toni's Treviso team. A few months later, at the age of 25, Toni Kukoč was gleaming with excitement as he donned a Chicago Bulls jersey. However, it all began in frustration, with Michael Jordan announcing his (temporary) retirement. In the 1994–1995 season, Kukoč emerged as the second-best player in the Illinois squad. The American public was stunned by his versatility. Rare for an outside player of this size, his specialty was drawing the defender towards him to create space in the paint. Then, in March 1995, there was great excitement: Air Jordan was back on the courts. That season, Kukoč was the best passer on 31 occasions.

Things went downhill two years later, with the arrival of Dennis Rodman, who sent Toni to the bench. He was still their third option in attack and, after all, the ultimate victory in the NBA Finals, against the Seattle SuperSonics, outweighed the annoyance. As in the European finals a few years earlier, Toni Kukoč hit a triple in the North American league's record book. After Jordan's definitive retirement, followed by the departures of Pippen and Rodman, Toni regained his place as offensive leader. In February 2000, he was propelled to the Philadelphia Sixers, but his new coach, Larry Brown, relegated him to the role of substitute, even though he still had excellent statistics.

A few months later, he moved to the Atlanta Hawks. Unfortunately, serious foot problems prevented him from finishing the season. Kukoč ended his career in the States with the Milwaukee Bucks. Far from those years in Chicago, Toni Kukoč didn't seem to get the recognition he deserved. His former teammate Bill Wellington regrets this. "We always talk about Jordan and Pippen with the Bulls, but Toni was really a pillar of our team." The Croatian, who had a hip operation in 2009 but is still keen on sport, took up golf and regularly crosses paths with Michael Jordan on the green. "I play with him for two dollars, and even then, it's a competition between us!"

DID YOU KNOW?

Toni Kukoč, who was selected 29th overall in the 1990 draft, was already on the Bulls' radar. However, the Croatian decided to stay at home in Split. War was brewing in Yugoslavia, and he wanted to be close to his family. Further, he was put off by the attitude of the haughty Americans, led by Michael Jordan, who did not even bother to watch his video. Scottie Pippen, in the middle of renegotiations to extend his contract, also wasn't keen on the arrival of a European competitor. Ever pragmatic, Kukoč waited three more seasons before arriving in Chicago.

Toni Kukoč (7) of the Milwaukee Bucks is fouled by Antonio McDyess (24) of the Detroit Pistons, at the Bradley Center in Milwaukee, April 17, 2006.

AUSTRALIA

Luc LONGLEY

BORN ON: 19 January 1969

IN: Melbourne

HEIGHT: 7'2" (2.18 m)

POSITION: Center

PROFESSIONAL CAREER: Perth Wildcats; Minnesota Timberwolves; Chicago Bulls; Phoenix Suns; New York Knicks

ACHIEVEMENTS: 3 NBA championship titles (1996, 1997, 1998)

Detroit Pistons' Jerry Stackhouse (42) tries to fight through a pick by Chicago Bulls' Luc Longley (13) as he guards Bulls' Ron Harper (9) on February 15, 1998, in Chicago.

A starter during the Chicago Bulls' second three-peat, Luc Longley never enjoyed the fame or prestige of Jordan, Pippen, or even Rodman. However, his role in those titles should not be underestimated, nor should his influence on international basketball, particularly in his native Australia. As the first player from his country to ever join the NBA, he paved the way for players such as Andrew Bogut, Josh Giddey, Patty Mills, Joe Ingles, and Ben Simmons.

DID YOU KNOW?

Luc Longley hardly features in the docu-series *The Last Dance*. So, the Australians and their center came up with a fun move – a kind of tongue-in-cheek response with his own documentary. Longley was the subject of an in-depth profile in *One Giant Leap*, which retraced his career and life, while evoking his absence from Netflix's global success.

NO GLITZ, EXCEPT FOR THE TITLES

Luc Longley was never a flashy or spectacular player, nor was he an elite scorer. He was a behind-the-scenes player, a team player, someone who was indispensable in the quest for an NBA title. The kind of player people tend to forget when it's time to hand out the credit. Yet it was difficult to overlook this 7-foot-2, 265-pound colossus, predestined by nature to play center. Admittedly, a center who never averaged more than 10 rebounds in a season and only once scored more than 10 points, in 1997–1998. But that didn't matter.

When he arrived in the United States in 1987, Luc Longley was still just a prospect from the Perth Wildcats, a team in the NBL, the Australian league. To make a name for himself, he spent four years playing for the University of New Mexico. Although not a starter in his first season in the US, Longley started almost every game in the following three years. In total, he played 132 games for the New Mexico Lobos, averaging 13.4 points, 7 rebounds, and 2.4 assists. More importantly, he averaged 2.5 blocks per game, including more than three in his last two years, while shooting almost 60 percent from the field and over 70 percent from the free throw line. These statistics made him a draft attraction, especially as his height was the stuff of dreams for NBA scouts. Luc entered the league when he was drafted seventh overall in the first round by the Minnesota Timberwolves. Unfortunately, the experience was short-lived, and in his third season he was sent to Chicago to play for the Bulls. This new team would bring him the greatest successes of his career. He didn't immediately become a starter, and it took him a year and a half to really establish himself in the starting five, where he remained until he left the Bulls in 1998. In Illinois, he benefited from Michael Jordan's return from retirement to win three consecutive championship rings, beating center Karl Malone twice (1997, 1998). In 1996, against the Sonics, he had his best finals, averaging 11.7 points, 3.8 rebounds, 2.2 assists, and 1.8 blocks.

A perfectionist, Luc Longley spent much longer dwelling on his failed final years in New York and Phoenix than on his successes in Illinois. It's true that after his triple crown, he was undoubtedly hoping for a bigger role in another franchise, where he could show that his achievements in Chicago weren't just down to the stars he played alongside. Except that nothing went as planned, and his statistics plummeted. By his own admission, the end of his career was "a nightmare." Troubled by a body that was starting to show signs of wear and tear, Longley said goodbye to the NBA courts.

As a result, Luc did not necessarily have fond memories of his years in the league, feeling uncomfortable about his injuries and his paychecks. "Getting paid without playing felt weird because you always want to earn your money," he said. "I accepted the money because that's the rule, but it was horrible. I was very sad." As an Australian national, Longley took the opportunity to compete in the Olympic games three times (1988, 1992, 2000), before later devoting himself to coaching the national team as an assistant coach. He was determined to give back to Australian basketball what it had given him throughout his career. With that adventure coming to an end in 2019, he is now an advisor to the NBL.

THE ETERNALLY FORGOTTEN

Luc Longley is absent from the globally successful documentary *The Last Dance*, because the producers didn't deem it necessary to interview him. Even so, he is very discreetly mentioned throughout the documentary series. His absence may have caused some speculation, but it also allowed Longley to return to the hearts of basketball fans, who became a little more interested in him and his story. Even Michael Jordan himself was moved by the fact that his former teammate did not appear in the documentary! For Longley, it was more than just a missed opportunity, as he never loses his great modesty: "Since they didn't interview me, I didn't really expect to be in it, even though I thought I might appear a little bit."

While it's clear that the center's record would have been very different had he

ON THIS DAY . . .

OCTOBER 8, 2009

Luc Longley was never selected to be inducted into the NBA Hall of Fame. However, a few others Halls of Fame have welcomed the former center into their ranks. This is particularly true of the Australian basketball Hall of Fame, but also of Australian sport as a whole. In 2009, the Sport Australia Hall of Fame celebrated Luc for his impact on basketball at home and his broader efforts to promote sport in Australia. A great way to pay him back – in the best sense.

not played alongside Michael Jordan in the late 1990s, Longley never hid his dislike for His Airness. Too tyrannical and even sometimes mean to his teammates, especially to the Australian for his lack of rebounding despite his height, Jordan was anything but easy to get along with. In 2021, Longley spoke candidly about his relationship with the star in a documentary for Australian television.

"You don't have to like a man to be on his team, care about him, and play basketball together," he said. It was a personal explanation that also showed that Longley was able to put his own opinions aside to win titles, just like the Bulls' No. 23.

LEFT: Phoenix Suns center Luc Longley (13) goes up for a basket against Indiana Pacers forward Sam Perkins (14), on January 25, 2000, in Indianapolis.

RIGHT: Australia's Luc Longley (13) battles for the ball with Yugoslavia's Željko Rebrača (11) on September 19, 2000.

Karl MALONE

BORN ON: 24 July 1963

IN: Summerfield, Louisiana

HEIGHT: 6′9″ (2.06 m)

POSITION: Power forward

PROFESSIONAL CAREER: Utah Jazz; Los Angeles Lakers

ACHIEVEMENTS: 2 Olympic gold medals (1992, 1996); 2 NBA regular season MVP titles (1997, 1999)

Karl Malone (32) attempts to score a basket during the Los Angeles Clippers-Utah Jazz NBA game at the Los Angeles Memorial Sport Arena, January 27, 1993.

A hard worker through and through, at the end of the group training session, Karl Malone would go off by himself to shoot free throws. At the beginning of his career, the Louisianan struggled to obtain a 50 percent success rate in this skill. Through constant repetition, 15 years later, it was around 75 percent. Over time, the power forward became the best scorer in this area, with 9,787 free throws made in 19 NBA seasons. His overall point tally reached a staggering 36,928 points, making him the league's third all-time scorer behind Kareem Abdul-Jabbar and LeBron James.

ON THIS DAY . . .

JANUARY 27, 1990

Annoyed at not being selected for the All-Star Game, Karl Malone went on a rampage in the wake of this setback. On January 27, 1990, for the Milwaukee Bucks' visit, the Mailman broke his NBA scoring record (61), with a success rate of 80 percent. This performance is even more impressive when you consider that Karl only played for 33 minutes. With such a show of strength, the Bucks were swept away by the Malone tsunami and the Utah Jazz won comfortably (144–96).

AGAINST ALL ODDS

In 18 years at the highest level with the Utah Jazz, from 1985 to 2003, Karl Anthony Malone missed just 10 games, three of which were due to suspension. Formidable and robust, like his role model Shaquille O'Neal, Karl Malone had a reputation for being a bruiser. A little too much sometimes. Impulsive, he was known to use defensive moves that should be banned in basketball schools.

Karl grew up on a farm in Summerfield, the youngest of nine children brought up tough by a mother. Karl was a teenager when his father died – a traumatic event for him and his whole family. Basketball was his one outlet, and, thanks to his size, he didn't go unnoticed.

His first thrills came in the paint, and his room was decorated with a host of college trophies he won while playing with the Louisiana Tech Bulldogs.

Then the age of innocence was over and, in the 1985 off-season, the draft loomed. Convinced he was on the Mavericks' radar, Karl Malone planned ahead and organized an apartment in the heart of Dallas. Then he ended up in Utah! At the last minute, the Texan franchise chose Detlef Schrempf over him. "I then decided to kick the Mavs' asses as soon as I crossed their path," Karl said, "because they lied to me. Every time, I want to destroy them!" With such a will to win, Malone quickly established himself on the Utah Jazz roster and, in his second season, became an essential leader on the court.

THE TRAIL BLAZERS SPOIL THE PARTY

At the beginning of 1988, Karl was selected for the All-Star Game, the first of a long series of 14 appearances. With his club, he discovered the playoffs but came up against the Lakers of Kareem Abdul-Jabbar and Magic Johnson. However, with an average of 30 points per game, Karl Malone inherited a beautiful nickname that best defined his consistency: "the Mailman," because he scored baskets at a steady pace like a mailman delivering mail.

Four years later, the Utah Jazz reached the Western Conference Finals for the first time, but Portland spoiled the party. Karl Malone consoled himself with the Olympic gold medal he brought back from Barcelona with the Dream Team. Then, the following season, the Utah Jazz won 60 games in their regular season, including 15 consecutive away games. It was even more convincing in 1996–1997 when the Salt Lake City team achieved the best campaign in its history – 64 wins and only 18 defeats – and Karl Malone was logically voted NBA player of the year. In addition to his power, Karl Malone stood out for his speed in blocking shots and constantly played the pick and roll, leaving even the top experts in awe.

Karl Malone and his teammates during the NBA game San Antonio Spurs-Los Angeles Lakers at the SBC Center in San Antonio, May 5, 2004.

THE BULLS AGAIN AND AGAIN

Michael Jordan's Chicago Bulls upset the fairytale journey, dominating the Jazz in the final. History repeated itself a year later. After starting the series at full speed,

Karl Malone during a match at the 1996 Atlanta Olympics.

Karl Malone was locked down by Scottie Pippen and Dennis Rodman. In Game 5, the Jazz power forward scored 39 points in an incredible feat in Chicago. During the decisive game at the Delta Center, the suspense became unbearable a few seconds before the verdict, but at the buzzer, the Bulls sealed the deal (83–81). A brutal ending that was hard to swallow and would have lasting effects.

Six months later, in November 1998, there was trouble between Karl Malone and his managers. After 18 years, the Mailman was ready to set sail. Not himself on the court, the Louisianan elbowed his Portland counterpart, Brian Grant, and had to pay a $10,000 fine.

For the 2003–2004 season, obsessed with the ultimate title, Karl Malone joined Kobe Bryant and Shaquille O'Neal at the Lakers. He was convinced the title was within reach, setting a triple-double record for a player over 40, but his body said stop. In the final against the Detroit Pistons, his knee gave out and the power forward resigned himself to surgery. Although his future in Los Angeles ended prematurely, all was not lost. The New York Knicks had their eye on the two-time Olympic champion, and the San Antonio Spurs kept the door open for him. But, faced with the inevitable, Karl Malone decided to announce the end of the adventure on February 13, 2005. To recharge his batteries, the Mailman returned to Louisiana to mentor the younger generation of Bulldogs.

DID YOU KNOW?

47 stitches! Even today, Isiah Thomas still hasn't gotten over the time that Karl Malone elbowed him on December 14, 1991, just as the Detroit Pistons point guard was about to reach the circle. With his eyebrow cut open, Thomas suffered massive bleeding above the eye. Karl Malone led with his elbow and made no effort to avoid the collision. "It's the worst move in the history of basketball," said the Michigan player. The Louisianan had to pay a modest fine of $1,000 and serve a one-game suspension.

Hakeem
OLAJUWON

BORN ON: 21 January 1963

IN: Lagos, Nigeria

HEIGHT: 7'0" (2.13 m)

POSITION: Center

PROFESSIONAL CAREER: Houston Rockets; Toronto Raptors

ACHIEVEMENTS: 2 NBA championship titles (1994, 1995); 1 NBA regular season MVP title (1994); 2 NBA Finals MVP titles (1994, 1995); 1 Olympic gold medal (1996)

Hakeem Olajuwon (34) of the Houston Rockets drives to the basket while being defended by Patrick Ewing (33) during a game against the New York Knicks at Madison Square Garden in 1989.

Imagine being so strong, so unpredictable, so elegant and, most of all, so technically gifted that people call you "the Dream". That's the story of Hakeem "the Dream" Olajuwon. Born in Lagos, Nigeria, Olajuwon had no real ambition to become a basketball star in his youth. A soccer fan, he focused on the other round ball until he was 15. As a goalkeeper, he developed skills that would serve him well in blocking shots, but his height caught the eye of basketball scouts and in 1980 he left Nigeria to join the Cougars at the University of Houston.

DID YOU KNOW?

In terms of versatility on the court, few have reached the same level as Olajuwon. He recorded a quadruple-double and holds the best average number of blocks per game in history, while also ranking in the top 10 for steals. These qualities enabled him to achieve six "five-by-fives" during his career, an NBA record! A "five-by-five" is when a player scores at least five points in each statistical category on a game sheet. In an era where triple-doubles are becoming more common, the rarity of a five-by-five speaks for itself.

A LEGACY AND MEMORIES THAT REMAIN INTACT

Although he spent four years at university in Houston, Hakeem only played for three seasons, due to administrative issues that prevented him from playing during his first year. He arrived in the city a complete stranger, to the point that no one came to pick him up at the airport. But that didn't matter, as things got off to a good start in his second year.

With Olajuwon, the Cougars reached the Final Four every year between 1981 and 1984, with two finals in 1983 and 1984, both of which they lost. This was impressive consistency in an NCAA where competition is fierce. Known for their "showtime" style and dunking, the Texans were nicknamed "Phi Slamma Jamma," in reference to the college's fraternities. Their game was unconventional, but it worked. It took James Worthy and Michael Jordan's North Carolina to knock them out in 1982 and 1983, and Patrick Ewing's Georgetown to block their path in 1984. Olajuwon left college with a hint of bitterness. Now he had to show the big league his finesse and his "dream shake."

A mix of all kinds of fakes, with constant use of his back to the basket, the "dream shake" was Olajuwon's signature move. Technical enough to fake out opponents in any position, mobile enough to leave them in the dust in a split second, and skilled enough to pull off a quick hook shot or a jump shot, Hakeem did whatever he wanted in the low post, and he owed it in part to his famous "dream shake." A lethal weapon, even in a golden era for NBA centers, it would prompt Shaquille O'Neal to shower him with compliments: "Hakeem has five moves, in which there are four other moves each time. So that gives him 20 moves in total."

USA's Hakeem Olajuwon (15) in action at the Atlanta Olympic Games in 1996.

DOMINATE, DOMINATE AND THEN BLOCK

At the age of 21, and with only four years of basketball under his belt, Hakeem was propelled to the top of the draft and among the country's greatest hopefuls, including the likes of Michael Jordan, Charles Barkley, and John Stockton. Simply being drafted ahead of the man considered by many to be the greatest player of all time, without having carried the burden for his entire career, could be enough to classify Hakeem's time in the league as a success. Unsurprisingly, Jordan showed everyone what kind of player he would be by dominating the league and winning the Rookie of the Year award . . . ahead of Olajuwon, the only other rookie to receive votes for the title. In fact, Olajuwon was already posting All-Star statistics, with 20.6 points, 11.9 rebounds, and 2.7 blocks, confirming Houston's decision to select him in their precious draft pick.

His talent was confirmed the following year. His statistics were even more impressive, and the Rockets even reached the NBA Finals! Except, in the final game, they had to face the Celtics and Larry Bird, and the task was still a little too daunting. The epic journey was over, but Olajuwon had already reached the finals in his second season. His partnership with Ralph Sampson was so promising that it was easy to imagine Houston as a regular title contender in the years to come. Unfortunately, Sampson's knees and some positive drug tests among his teammates quickly put an end to Texas's hopes. Sampson was traded and Houston put all its money on Olajuwon.

Hakeem became the player everyone was hoping for, racking up season after season of dominance. Although the Rockets sometimes struggled to make the playoffs, the Nigerian was not to blame. Especially since it was the Lakers and the Celtics who dominated the league in his early days, followed by Michael Jordan's Bulls, who crushed the competition. But when Jordan decided to retire, Olajuwon seized the opportunity and reached the NBA Finals the following

Houston Rockets' Hakeem Olajuwon (34) shoots on Boston Celtics' Robert Parish (00) and Reggie Lewis (35) at Boston Garden in 1988.

season. Facing Patrick Ewing's Knicks, he refused to relive the disappointment of the college championship and carried Houston to victory, winning by just six points. For Olajuwon, the Finals MVP trophy was a foregone conclusion, as he was the best player in the series.

The following season, the Rockets went on to win a second consecutive title. In the final against Orlando, Olajuwon crushed a young Shaquille O'Neal, and the Rockets swept the Magic. Naturally, he was voted MVP of the Finals. In that playoff campaign, Hakeem dominated Karl Malone, Charles Barkley, David Robinson, and Shaq, four Hall of Famers standing in his way. His 725 points scored in a single postseason remains the fourth-highest total in history. Olajuwon would never return to the finals, but the main thing was that he was champion – and not just once, but twice! A few less successful years followed, and Olajuwon ended his illustrious career with a forgettable season with the Toronto Raptors in 2001–2002, finally retiring due to back problems. Naturalized as an American citizen in 1993, he even had the opportunity to win Olympic gold with Team USA at the 1996 Olympic Games in Atlanta. Just to add a little more to the American "Dream."

In 18 seasons in the league, Olajuwon dominated almost every year, and of course, broke more than one barrier or record. The first non-American to be an All-Star and start in the game, the first non-American MVP or Defensive Player of the Year – those are the achievements tied to his roots.

ON THIS DAY . . .

MARCH 9, 1991

Born Akeem, Olajuwon officially changed his first name to Hakeem on March 9, 1991. Like Lew Alcindor, who became Kareem Abdul-Jabbar, Olajuwon embraced Islam more deeply, even though he was raised Muslim in Nigeria. He was known for his study of the Quran, which brought wisdom to the court, where he could sometimes be a temperamental player. A major figure of Islam in the United States, he has sometimes helped promote a positive image of the religion, particularly in Texas. Despite his tough NBA schedule, he always observed Ramadan, game or not, and was even named Player of the Month in February 1995, the month of Ramadan.

UNITED STATES

Shaquille

O'NEAL

BORN ON: 6 March 1972

IN: Newark, New Jersey

HEIGHT: 7'1" (2.16 m)

POSITION: Center

PROFESSIONAL CAREER: Orlando Magic; Los Angeles Lakers; Miami Heat; Phoenix Suns; Cleveland Cavaliers; Boston Celtics

ACHIEVEMENTS: 1 Olympic gold medal (1996); 1 World Championship title (1994); 4 NBA Championship titles (2000, 2001, 2002, 2006); 1 NBA regular season MVP title (2000); 3 NBA Finals MVP titles (2000, 2001, 2002)

Shaquille O'Neal during the NBA game Boston Celtics-Toronto Raptors, November 22, 2010.

When Shaq takes flight to aim for the hoop, he sends it way over the top. Since his NBA debut in 1992, Shaquille O'Neal has blown two backboards, which were smashed to smithereens by one of his slam dunks. Faced with the size and impact of the then-new Orlando center, the NBA had to take action and reinforce supports and panels with composite materials more likely to withstand his weight.

DID YOU KNOW?

Shaquille O'Neal is one of only three NBA players who, in the same season, won the title of MVP in the regular season, the NBA Finals, and the All-Star Game. Shaq achieved this historic triple feat in 2000, joining Willis Reed, center for the New York Knicks, who achieved this success in 1970, and the legendary Michael Jordan, who won these awards twice with the Chicago Bulls, in 1996 and 1998.

AN EXCEPTIONAL PHYSIQUE

At the age of 12, Shaq was already 6 foot 6 (1.98 m). A few years later, he crossed paths with a certain Dale Brown, the basketball coach at Louisiana State University, who immediately recognized the young man's potential. After finishing high school, Shaq would go on to play for the LSU Tigers. Three years later, the Orlando Magic snapped up the colossus in the making. After waiting two seasons, Orlando reached the NBA Finals after knocking out Michael Jordan's Chicago Bulls. But Shaq stumbled over the final hurdle, Hakeem Olajuwon's Houston Rockets.

The following summer, Shaq arrived at the Los Angeles Lakers with a newcomer who already had a strong reputation, Kobe Bryant. After a laborious start, O'Neal took advantage of coach Phil Jackson's arrival on the bench to truly find his full potential in the game.

But Shaq waited until 1999–2000 to really reach the stars. In addition to his huge frame, Shaquille O'Neal was adept at a few moves that would make him a legend, such as the jump hook, that delightful arm roll, and the drop step, when he attacked with his back to the basket before pivoting to score. In 2000, the NBA Finals were won at the expense of Reggie Miller's Indiana Pacers. In the opening game, Shaquille O'Neal scored 43 points and 19 rebounds.

It was Shaq's golden age, and he was on a roll, winning two more titles in quick succession. Experts would call this anthology treble the "three-peat." With its Fantastic Four (Kobe Bryant, Karl Malone, Gary Payton, and Shaquille O'Neal), there were high hopes for the Lakers' 2003–2004 season. The fans were soon to be disappointed. Right from the start, tensions between Black Mamba and Shaq weakened the team's foundations. After the

defeat in the final against the Detroit Pistons, the divorce was finalized and, in the 2004 off-season, Shaq decided to go and dunk under other skies.

FROM MIAMI . . .

Miami Heat was his new home, and O'Neal reclaimed the number 32 he had worn in Orlando. The Herculean center was back in action under the basket, so much so that, for the ninth time in his career, he was top in field goal percentage, joining the legendary Wilt Chamberlain in this honorary ranking. On the diplomatic front, it was time to reconcile with Kobe Bryant, and the two men shook hands again when they met.

In the 2006 NBA Finals, the Heat were initially outplayed by the Dallas Mavericks, losing the first two games, before Shaq and his teammates pulled out the daggers to claim the title (4– 2). A short-lived bright spell, as Miami suffered a terrible slump the following season. Shaq's average dropped to 14 points per game. The crash came in the first round of the playoffs, against the Chicago Bulls.

Aware that he was clearly slowing down, Shaq committed to a strict regimen to regain a healthy weight more in line with top-level sport. On the court, Ricky Davis's contribution in attack also helped him. Despite all this, Shaq no longer had the same influence on the group, and he was not even selected for the All-Star Game, an unprecedented event in his career. However, Shaq did not feel he was on the wane and even boasted: "If I were a painter, you would call me 'Shaqcasso'!" In February 2008, against the New York Knicks, the master reached the symbolic milestone of 25,000 points scored in the NBA.

. . . TO PHOENIX

With frequent knee injuries and a falling out with coach Pat Riley, Shaq left Miami for the Phoenix Suns. Ever ambitious, Shaq lost even more weight to be faster, make fewer mistakes, and make more passes. In February 2009, Shaq took part in his 15th All-Star Game, then completed two games with over 30 points, something he hadn't done in five years. His stint with the Cleveland Cavaliers and his pairing with LeBron James felt like the final chapter in his basketball legacy. But Shaquille O'Neal bought himself a bonus season with the Boston Celtics.

Physically diminished, the titan played just 37 matches for the Celtics. On June 1, 2011, Shaq announced his retirement and the media went wild. As did the numbers – 28,596 points, 13,099 rebounds, and over 3,026 assists.

ON THIS DAY . . .

MARCH 6, 2000

Happy birthday, Shaq! On his 28th birthday, March 6, 2000, Shaquille O'Neal gave himself a nice birthday present. Against the Los Angeles Clippers, the center went on a scoring binge, dropping 61 points – the highest total for a center in the NBA since Wilt Chamberlain. Not content with this achievement, Shaq also managed 23 rebounds in 45 minutes of play. "Phil Jackson preferred to take me off because he didn't want me to overtake Michael Jordan," Shaq quipped, before concluding: "Afterwards, I went out partying anyway."

Shaquille O'Neal at the Phoenix Suns-Denver Nuggets NBA game, April 1, 2008.

FRANCE

Tony PARKER

BORN ON: 17 May 1982

IN: Bruges, Belgium

HEIGHT: 6'2" (1.88 m)

POSITION: Point guard

PROFESSIONAL CAREER: Paris Basket Racing; San Antonio Spurs; ASVEL Lyon-Villeurbanne; San Antonio Spurs; Charlotte Hornets

ACHIEVEMENTS: 1 Euro Championship title (2013); 4 NBA championship titles (2003, 2005, 2007, 2014); 1 NBA Finals MVP title (2007)

Tony Parker's (9) dunk during the Miami Heat-San Antonio Spurs NBA game, January 17, 2012.

Born in Belgium to a Dutch mother and an American father, ending up as a French national, Tony Parker has an incredible story. Originally from Chicago, his father, Tony Senior, was an excellent defender in the States before embarking on a career in Europe, first in the Netherlands, then in Belgium. The Parker family settled in Normandy, France, where Tony Junior signed on with USF Fécamp, his first official club, and began making a name for himself on the court.

ON THIS DAY . . .

JANUARY 15, 2019

On January 15, 2019, when Tony Parker joined the Charlotte Hornets for a final season as a pro, he became the first and only player in history to have a positive record against all 30 NBA franchises. In this tally, the French point guard is ahead of legends such as Tim Duncan, Manu Ginobili, David Robinson, Magic Johnson, and James Worthy. The franchise bested that evening was none other than the San Antonio Spurs, who were dominated by the Hornets (108–93), to the great displeasure of a certain Gregg Popovich, Tony's former coach in Texas.

FOR THE LOVE OF THE JERSEY

One thing is clear – the future Spurs point guard has always had a sincere love for the French national team jersey. "I'm so proud to play for my country," he maintained throughout his career, to silence certain skeptics convinced that Tony Parker's American roots would eventually take over.

Naturally, Tony Senior was a firm believer in his son's talent. From high school and beyond, Tony Junior amazed everyone with his ease under the hoop. This time, at the age of 15, a decision was made. Not only did the prodigy opt for an American passport, but he also joined the Federal Basketball Center at the National Institute of Sport, Expertise, and Performance in Paris.

This didn't stop the teenager from wallpapering his bedroom with Michael Jordan posters. Tony was on the cusp of adulthood when he joined PSG Racing, where he was then only a replacement on the bench. Yet, already, his lively passing, his ease of getting into the paint, not to mention his shooting success, left people wanting more.

A CRAZY BET

At the time of the 2001 draft, Tony Parker was obsessed with the NBA. The only problem was that hardly anyone in the US was interested in a European point guard. From his modest 28th place, TP could hardly show off. His first tryout with the San Antonio Spurs was a fiasco. "I messed up during this tryout in Chicago, and Gregg Popovich, my future coach, said, 'I don't want this point guard, he's useless!'" Parker hid his frustration, didn't get discouraged, and went back to Texas. This time, the Spurs signed the French hopeful. Even so, he still had a long way

to go to make a name for himself. San Antonio's star at the time was the giant Tim Duncan. At 6 foot 11 (2.11 m), he didn't even deign to speak to the runt Tony Parker. "I knew I had to earn his respect," recalled Parker. "Basketball is everything in the United States, so I knew I had to prove myself."

Then the Spurs' fortunes changed, and Tony Parker even became the darling of Popovich, a master strategist who was finally won over by the spectacular qualities and charisma of his point guard. Tony Parker reached new heights and became one of the key players of the North American seasons. Everything fell into place.

Tony Parker (9) at the NBA Europe Live San Antonio Spurs-Maccabi Tel Aviv game in Paris, October 8, 2006.

TIME FOR REVIEW

From 2006, Tony Parker became the first French player to win an NBA Finals title, and then to participate in an All-Star Game! He became a celebrity, including in his private life, due to his relationship with his ***Desperate Housewives*** actress Eva Longoria. Despite his success in Texas, Tony Parker didn't perform as well with the French national team. He did win the bronze medal at Euro 2005, but his record with Les Bleus is much more mixed, and TP was frustrated.

It would take eight more seasons before the French team triumphed on the continent, after a final victory in Slovenia against Lithuania (80–66). With the French flag draped over his shoulders,

France's victory over Lithuania in the final of the European basketball championship. From left to right, front row: Nicolas Batum, Nando De Colo, Tony Parker, Florent Piétrus, Boris Diaw, in Ljubljana, Slovenia, September 22, 2013.

DID YOU KNOW?

When he joined ASVEL in the fall of 2011, taking advantage of the NBA lockout, Tony Parker was doing what he loved. So much so that his base salary with the Rhône-based team was set at just 1,500 euros per month! The Spurs point guard even admits to paying for his insurance out of his own pocket so as not to weigh down the Villeurbanne payroll too much. "Playing with Ronny Turiaf in France was really great," he said of his time with the team. "Everywhere we went, it was crazy. We were a bit like the Beatles! Whether it was in Cholet, Le Havre, or Strasbourg, it was really fun."

Tony Parker bellowed out the French national anthem on the podium.

In 2018, after 17 years with the Spurs (with a stint at ASVEL in 2011–2012), Tony Parker finished his lap of honor with the Charlotte Hornets.

Naturally, as soon as he hung up his jersey, the former point guard headed back to France, but he didn't cut ties with the basketball world. In 2014, he became president of the Villeurbanne club, where he brings his strategic flair for sports and business.

UNITED STATES

Scottie

PIPPEN

BORN ON: 25 September 1965

IN: Hamburg, Arkansas

HEIGHT: 6′8″ (2.03 m)

POSITION: Forward

PROFESSIONAL CAREER: Chicago Bulls; Houston Rockets; Portland Trail Blazers; Chicago Bulls; Torpan Pojat Helsinki; Sundsvall Dragons

ACHIEVEMENTS: 2 Olympic gold medals (1992, 1996); 6 NBA championship titles (1991, 1992, 1993, 1996, 1997, 1998)

Scottie Pippen (33) of the Chicago Bulls surrounded by his Detroit Pistons opponents during the NBA game at Chicago Stadium, November 11, 1992.

From the ToPo (Torpan Pojat Helsinki) to the Dragons, Scottie Pippen gave himself an astonishing epilogue in 2007–2008. The former Bulls forward decided to round off his hitherto flawless career with a quirky early retirement in Scandinavia. Was it worthy of a champion of his caliber, who had just spent 17 seasons in the NBA, to end his journey in this way?

A REMARKABLE RECORD

Sixteen successive appearances in the playoffs, six titles won with Chicago, and seven appearances in the All-Star Game. With a resume like that, "Pip" is one of only four players to have had his number retired by the Chicago Bulls.

Like many of the NBA's greats, the Arkansas prodigy's childhood wasn't an easy one. Coming from humble beginnings, Scottie got by with a modest scholarship to Hamburg High School. Initially a point guard, Scottie changed positions when he arrived at the University of Central Arkansas. It was there that he caught the eye of NBA scouts. At the age of 21, he stepped it up a notch, participating in the 1987 draft.

After some sleight of hand, involving a trade with the Seattle SuperSonics for Haitian center Olden Polynice, Pip ended up with the Chicago Bulls.

He made his NBA debut in November 1987 against the Philadelphia 76ers (winning 104–94). Pippen hung on every word of the absolute master, Michael Jordan, and with his advice, gave the impression of having three or four years of experience. Relieved to remain in the shadow of the New York guard, Pip was even proud to stay in his place. "I would never want to be Michael Jordan. People jump all over him as soon as he appears. For me, it's quieter with the fans."

In November 1990, during a demonstration against the Los Angeles Clippers, Scottie achieved his first triple-double. He helped the Bulls achieve the first three-peat in their history, winning three championships in a row, from 1991 to 1993. His influence in the system set up by coach Phil Jackson was more decisive than it seemed. Wearing the gold medal around his neck after the 1992 Olympic tournament in Barcelona gave Pip an even bigger boost. The following year, Michael Jordan's

ON THIS DAY . . .

OCTOBER 2, 1999

False start on October 2, 1999! Announced as joining the Los Angeles Lakers, where he dreamed of meeting up again with his favorite coach from the Bulls, Phil Jackson, Scottie Pippen actually ended up in Portland. From California to Oregon, the leap was surprising all the same. During the transaction, Pip was traded for no less than six Trail Blazers players! In four seasons in Portland, Pip would play a total of 272 games with the Trail Blazers.

retirement could have marked a halt or a break, but Scottie Pippen rolled up his sleeves and took over from His Airness.

Everything would have worked out perfectly if an incident had not occurred in May 1994. In the middle of the Eastern Conference semifinal against the Knicks, in a last-ditch move, coach Phil Jackson asked Toni Kukoč to take charge, leaving Scottie Pippen on the sidelines. A blatant insult! Pippen was happy to take a back seat to Jordan, but he couldn't stand being left with the scraps behind a Croatian rookie, and he flew into a memorable rage. His departure seemed inevitable in 1994, but in a twist of fate, he ended up staying. The return of Michael Jordan, combined with the arrival of Dennis Rodman, gave him a new lease on life.

Scottie Pippen (8) and Michael Jordan (9) try to influence the ball's trajectory during the USA-Croatia match at the Barcelona Summer Olympic Games, August 8, 1992.

THE LAST DANCE

Two seasons later, a new NBA title and the top step of the podium at the Atlanta Olympics restored his power under the basket. In February 1997, Scottie set his personal points record against the Denver Nuggets, scoring 47 points (winning 134–123). A few weeks later, in the final against the Utah Jazz, Pip was a hit and his performances in the clutch time flirted with the sublime. In the off-season, the hype subsided with

Scottie Pippen dribbles during a game at Madison Square Garden, New York, September 1, 1996.

DID YOU KNOW?

Scottie Pippen is the only player in the history of the NBA to have won two titles in the same year as two Olympic crowns won with the national team.
In 1992, he won the championship ring in the final against the Portland Trail Blazers, before winning Olympic gold in Barcelona during the summer with the Dream Team. He did it again four years later. Victorious in the 1996 finals against the Seattle SuperSonics, the forward from Arkansas was crowned at the Atlanta Games, after a straightforward win against Yugoslavia (95–69).

the departure of Phil Jackson and the definitive retirement of Michael Jordan. This end of the dynasty would be titled "The Last Dance" by NBA fans.

The following year, after 11 seasons with the Bulls, Scottie Pippen was traded to the Houston Rockets. His debut in Texas was mixed and, not really on the same wavelength as his new coach Charles Barkley, the Arkansas ace waited until the 1999–2000 season to regain his full influence. His transfer to Portland was a big help. Pippen tirelessly transformed the Trail Blazers' game from week to week, even to the point of taking them to the finals – which they lost – against Kobe Bryant and Shaquille O'Neal's Lakers.

The months following this relative failure looked bleak. Suffering from tendonitis in his right elbow, Scottie underwent surgery in early 2001. In an attempt to restore his reputation, he returned to the Bulls a few months later. But it was difficult to resurrect the past, even if Chicago once again welcomed him with open arms. Plagued by injuries, Pippen played just 23 games that season.

On February 2, 2004, number 33 definitively retired his NBA jersey after a defeat against the Seattle SuperSonics (97–109). Always very close to Michael Jordan, Pippen returned to the Bulls in 2010 as an ambassador for the franchise. Scottie Pippen would fulfill this mission for 10 years, before being dismissed and disappearing discreetly. As on the court, Pip did not want to make waves. He now leaves it up to his son, Scotty Junior, a point guard with the Memphis Grizzlies, to take up the torch and make a name for himself.

UNITED STATES

David ROBINSON

BORN ON: 6 August 1965

IN: Key West, Florida

HEIGHT: 7'1" (2.16 m)

POSITION: Center

PROFESSIONAL CAREER: San Antonio Spurs

ACHIEVEMENTS: 2 NBA championship titles (1999, 2003); 1 NBA regular season MVP title (1995); 2 Olympic gold medals (1992, 1996); 1 Olympic bronze medal (1988); 1 World Championship title (1986); 1 NBA Citizenship Award (2003)

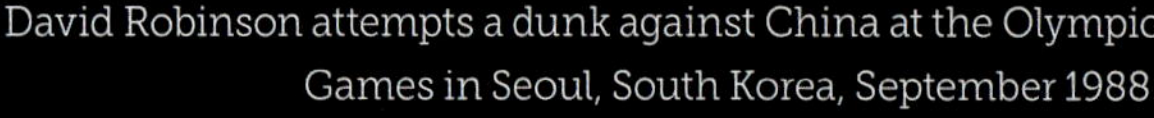

David Robinson attempts a dunk against China at the Olympic Games in Seoul, South Korea, September 1988.

The6 Afirst choice of the 1987 draft, David Robinson had to complete his military service before joining the NBA, so it took two years for him to play his first minutes in the league. It was an endless and almost unprecedented wait, but one that ultimately proved the Texas franchise right to take a chance on him, as it may well have laid the foundations for its contemporary success on that patience.

AYE, AYE, ADMIRAL!

Now considered one of the best franchises of the 21st century, the Spurs had yet to taste the joys of the Larry O'Brien Trophy when they selected David Robinson in the first pick of the 1987 draft. It was a logical choice, given how dominant the young center had been in his career so far.

The son of a military man, David was not a great basketball player in his youth, and was even rather detached from the game, preferring other sports. At only 5 foot 9 (1.75 m) as a teenager, he suddenly shot up when he turned 18, quickly approaching 6 foot 5 (1.96 m), which caught the attention of his high school's basketball coach, despite his lack of experience in the paint. He continued to grow, and in college he reached a height of 7 foot 1 (2.16 m), which he combined with impressive muscles. Robinson studied math at the United States Naval Academy, where basketball became part of his life. He led the team to March Madness, qualifying for the quarterfinals in 1986, and was even named best college player in 1987. A candidate for the NBA draft that same year, he was selected first overall by the San Antonio Spurs. It seemed like the start of a great career – just with a bit of a delay, because the young Robinson still had two years of compulsory service to complete in the Navy. Too tall and certainly too broad to be assigned to Navy ships, he was appointed as an engineer in the civilian service.

On November 4, 1989, having already won the Olympic gold medal with Team USA in Seoul, Robinson finally played his first minutes in the NBA. The result was astonishing. Against the Lakers, who had won three consecutive finals and two titles, Robinson dominated and the Spurs won. Some 23 points, 17 rebounds, and 3 blocks later, Robinson had silenced all doubts. The Spurs had waited for him, and it certainly paid off.

DID YOU KNOW?

Retiring from the courts in 2003, David Robinson didn't waste any time once he hung up his sneakers. As an investor, he has been able to grow his fortune through various businesses with a primarily social purpose. He was successful enough, in any case, to become a minority shareholder in the Spurs in 2004. This allowed him to continue contributing to the success of his longtime franchise while benefitting personally. His 1.88 percent stake is now worth just over $40 million.

His rookie season ended with the Rookie of the Year trophy, and he was invited to the All-Star event in his first season and for the next six seasons. The Spurs even won 35 more games than the previous season, regaining their status as one of the league's top teams.

This marked the beginning of a long reign for "the Admiral." His left hand was surprisingly refined for his size, and he boasted an unlimited offensive repertoire. For seven years, he racked up at least 23 points and 10 rebounds every game, carrying the Spurs through the vast majority of their games. In 1995, he was named MVP as he averaged 27.6 points, 10.8 rebounds, 2.9 assists, 3.2 blocks, and 1.6 steals per game. San Antonio was one of the best teams in the country and had every reason to believe it could win the title, but the Texan franchise still failed to make it past the playoffs.

David Robinson in action at the 1996 Olympics in Atlanta, Georgia.

To make matters worse, David was injured during the 1996–1997 season, and the Spurs plummeted as the Admiral played only six games. San Antonio's record was disastrous, and the draft and first picks were up for grabs, 10 years to the day after Robinson. The first pick landed in Texas, and Tim Duncan was the lucky winner. The duo of Robinson and Duncan became known as the "Twin Towers" – they were was unbeatable. The ultimate reward soon followed. The Spurs crushed the New York Knicks in the finals, And Robinson was finally an NBA champion! With Duncan at his side, Robinson's stats decreased, but it didn't matter. The Spurs had a future, and the Admiral had his successor. When Duncan considered jumping ship for the Orlando Magic during his first free agency in the summer of 2000, Robinson encouraged

David Robinson of the San Antonio Spurs (left) versus Shaquille O'Neal of the Orlando Magic, 1993.

ON THIS DAY . . .

Not content with having achieved a quadruple-double a few months earlier, David Robinson fought hard in April 1994 to be crowned the league's top scorer. In a battle with Shaquille O'Neal, he had to score as many points as possible to overtake his rival. And he did it in style! With the help of his teammates, who constantly set him up, Robinson crushed the Clippers and scored an incredible 71 points, shooting 26 out of 41 from the field. It's a franchise record that still stands today.

him to stay. Time would prove him right. In fact, even after Robinson announced his retirement at the end of the year 2002, the Spurs went on to win a second ring in 2003. After a masterful and unflinching performance in the finals, the Admiral retired with a second championship and all the fanfare.

FOUR FOR FOUR

During the 1993–1994 season, David Robinson was completely unguardable. With averages of 29.8 points and 10.7 rebounds per game, he was on another level. He scored 71 points on the final day of the regular season (see "On this day"), but more importantly, he achieved one of only four quadruple-doubles ever recorded in the league. On the evening of February 17, 1994, against the Detroit Pistons, the Admiral scored 34 points, before reaching precisely 10 in each of the following statistical categories: rebounds, assists, and blocks. His hyperactivity on the court allowed him to stay on for 43 minutes without overexerting himself, taking "only" 20 shots. But at that point, the Spurs didn't need much more to win by nearly 20 points for their 11th consecutive victory. Robinson ended his stellar performance on the free throw line, moments after recording a historic 10th block. Without getting carried away, he still savored this achievement, which was far from ordinary or insignificant. "I've been close to a quadruple-double several times," he said. "It's something I wanted to do. I'm happy because it's something you can never be sure you're going to achieve."

UNITED STATES

Dennis

RODMAN

BORN ON: 13 May 1961

IN: Trenton, New Jersey

HEIGHT: 6′7″ (2.01 m)

POSITION: Forward/ Power forward

PROFESSIONAL CAREER: Detroit Pistons; San Antonio Spurs; Chicago Bulls; Los Angeles Lakers; Dallas Mavericks

ACHIEVEMENTS: 5 NBA championship titles (1989, 1990, 1996, 1997, 1998)

Dennis Rodman at the San Antonio Spurs-New York Knicks NBA game at the Alamodome in San Antonio, November 17, 1993.

It goes without saying that Dennis Rodman definitely left his mark on basketball and popular culture more broadly. Wild as can be, the ultimate eccentric player, renowned for his antics both on and off the court, "Demolition Man" was especially known for his distinctive looks. Tattoos, piercings, and colorful hair dye go hand in hand with his performances.

A PROVOCATEUR AT HEART, BUT THAT'S NOT ALL

Make no mistake, the power forward was not just a provocateur – he was foremost a formidable defender who, on seven consecutive occasions between 1992 and 1998, was voted best rebounder. Not to mention his two NBA Defensive Player of the Year awards. Dennis Keith Rodman's five rings won with the Pistons and then the Bulls also earned him a place in the Hall of Fame. And to think that in high school, he was incapable of achieving a single layup. Held back by rough technique, for a long time he was left on the bench.

Rodman's early years bordered on complete destitution, with a Vietnam veteran father totally absent from his upbringing. Dennis hung out on the streets, where drugs and crime were rife. After high school, he made a living from odd jobs in the Oak Cliff neighborhood near Dallas. On the verge of being homeless, he accepted a job as a night watchman at the Fort Worth airport. It was then that he experienced a sudden growth spurt, rapidly growing from 5 foot 11 (1.80 m) to 6 foot 7 (2.01 m).

Almost by chance, he was spotted by the head basketball coach of Cooke County College, and although Rodman would flunk out after one semester, he demonstrated enough skill to be picked up by the team at Southeastern Oklahoma State University.

When it comes to basketball, SOSU isn't really anything to get excited about. Rodman wasn't bothered by this, especially as his exploits were few and far between. But he soon discovered that his specialty was rebounding. He became a dog on defense, aggressive in all circumstances, and just as radical at the other end of the court to create screens in attacking phases. In 1986, his team went to the NAIA semifinals, where Rodman scored an impressive 46 points in a single game, attracting attention from

ON THIS DAY . . .

JANUARY 25, 2000

For his last challenge at the highest level, on January 25, 2000, Dennis Rodman signed a contract with the Dallas Mavericks. At the age of 38, he returned to the Texas megalopolis where, as a child, he had more than his fair share of suffering. Revenge was short-lived, as Demolition Man had a run-in with franchise president Marc Cuban. Rodman only played 12 matches there. After his departure, Rodman delivered a scathing analysis of the Mavericks: "They need a point guard, a shooter, a power forward, a center, and a new owner but, other than that, they're ready!"

NBA scouts. Now eligible for the draft, Rodman was picked up by the Detroit Pistons as the 27th overall pick. Right from his NBA debut, "Rodzilla" was a real pain for his opponents. Even Atlanta Hawks forward Dominique Wilkins complained: "He's the most detestable player ever. He tears you down physically and mentally! "

In 1992, "Dennis the Menace" finished the season with 18.7 rebounds per game, the highest average since Wilt Chamberlain 20 years earlier. Despite his first titles and the recognition of his peers, even with his provocations, Rodman had a hard time coping with the departure of Chuck Daly, the Pistons' star coach who had become his mentor. What might appear to have been just another incident turned into a tragedy. His life began spinning out of control. He married and got divorced after only 83 days. Suffering from profound unhappiness, Dennis was even close to suicide.

Dennis Rodman is held back by teammate Michael Jordan, during the game against the Miami Heat at Miami Arena, during the 1996–1997 season.

A CAREER ON THE TIGHTROPE

He only has himself to thank for the wake-up call. Rodman decided to "kill the impostor" that lurked inside him. He changed his outlook, and a move to

Dennis Rodman (10) of the San Antonio Spurs in action against the Utah Jazz at the Delta Center in Salt Lake City, April 14, 1994.

DID YOU KNOW?

Despite his reputation, Dennis Rodman's disciplinary record is not catastrophic. In 911 NBA games over the course of his career, the bad boy was penalized 212 times for technical fouls, but, on the other hand, he was only sent off five times. It's worth noting that in the 1980s and 1990s, refereeing was more permissive. In March 1996, Rodman was still fined $20,000 and suspended for six matches, after feigning a headbutt at a referee.

the San Antonio Spurs gave his career a temporary boost. After a calmer period, he helped San Antonio become one of the league's top teams. But, it's easy to fall back into old habits . . .

After a motorcycle accident, Rodman dislocated a shoulder and missed 49 matches in a row. On his return, he began to slack off in training. Even so, in the 1995 off-season Chicago was trying to woo him. Still, the Bulls' Scottie Pippen wasn't keen on the arrival of Dennis the Menace. Ever the provocateur, he dropped his usual number 10, already taken when he arrived at the Bulls, for 91 . . . but he had to pay a fine, as the league doesn't allow any jersey number higher than 90!

In the 1998 climax, Rodman scored two decisive free throws, even though it's not his favorite skill. "Things aren't moving enough," said a rebellious Rodman. "It's way too static, but if I have to use them, I will!" At 38, he had no qualms about becoming the Lakers' luxury understudy to a sovereign Shaquille O'Neal. That didn't stop him from publicly sparring with his coach Kurt Rambis, who couldn't stand his lack of discipline.

Even so, by the end of his 15-year career, Dennis Rodman had racked up 11,954 rebounds. But that's not the end of the story. In March 2012, the *Los Angeles Times* claimed that the former forward was broke and an alcoholic. Yet he was seen on the courts in Mexico, then in the ABA, a parallel league in the States, before being spotted again in . . . North Korea! Rodman was there to promote basketball in the country, and even befriended its leader, Kim Jong-Un, in the process.

UNITED STATES

Bill
RUSSELL

BORN ON: 12 February 1934 in Monroe, Louisiana

DIED ON: 31 July 2022 in Mercer Island, Washington State

HEIGHT: 6'10" (2.08 m)

POSITION: Center

PROFESSIONAL CAREER: Boston Celtics

ACHIEVEMENTS: 1 Olympic gold medal (1956); 11 NBA championship titles (1957, 1959–1966, 1968, 1969); 5 NBA MVP titles (1958, 1961, 1962, 1963, 1965)

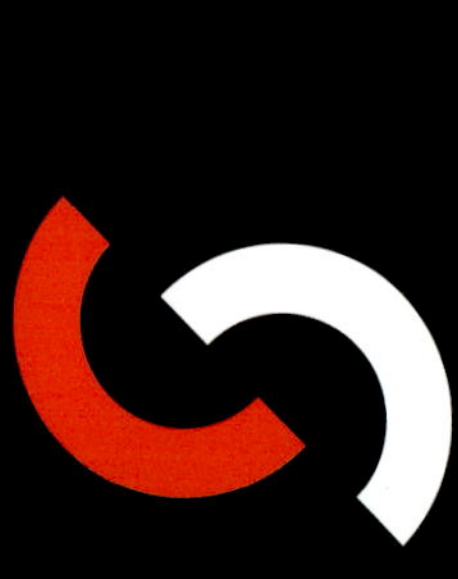

Bill Russell against the Philadelphia 76ers, December 13, 1963.

In terms of achievements, William "Bill" Russell is at the top of the pyramid. The center holds the all-time record for the number of NBA titles won, with eleven championships. A feat accomplished with a single franchise, the Boston Celtics. In his last three professional seasons, the man nicknamed the "Good Lord" even took on the dual role of player and coach. In 1966, Russell became the very first Black man to manage a league club, just two years after the abolition of segregation laws in the United States. Another victory for this Southerner, tormented throughout his life by racism and exclusion.

DID YOU KNOW?

Bill Russell's rivalry with Wilt Chamberlain didn't only exist in the courts – they also faced off on the asphalt. "I used to drive a Lamborghini 400 GT with the seat as far back as it would go, so I couldn't touch the pedals," said Russell. "Don't ask me who won the races with Wilt. You already know the answer . . ." Not sure Chamberlain would have agreed with this version of events.

BETWEEN HATRED, TOUGH LOVE, AND RESPECT RESPECT

A true warrior on the courts, Bill Russell may never have been an offensive leader, but over the course of his career, he still allowed himself the luxury of scoring a total of 14,522 points for the Celts in 1,128 games played (963 in the regular season and 165 in the playoffs).

Along with his rival Wilt Chamberlain, Russell is the only player to post an impressive total of over 50 rebounds in a game, having pulled down 21,620 in his career. And yet, before entering the arena, Bill Russell's legs often turned to jelly. Prone to nerve-induced stomach pains, it wasn't unusual for the Celtics center to vomit before an NBA game.

"He has a neurotic need to win," said his teammate, Tom Heinsohn. Bill had such a need for recognition that he put maximum pressure on himself. When you've grown up in the Deep South, with the Ku Klux Klan lurking about, it's hard to escape fear and its retrospective anxieties.

Son of Katie and Charles, young William was far from spoiled in his childhood. To escape postwar poverty, the family moved from Louisiana to California when Bill was eight, but he lost his mother in his early teens. His father got a job in a steel mill so he could better care for his children. Bill discovered basketball at McClymonds High School in Oakland, but he didn't really master the rules. Thanks to his long limbs, he felt more at home on the high jump.

BASKETBALL, THE ONLY WAY OUT

In the 1956 draft, Celtics coach Red Auerbach was captivated by the debonair college student. But the managers still needed to be convinced to sign him because his offensive stats were only average. What's more, it all became a mess when Bill Russell ended up signing with the Boston franchise just as he was about to fly to Melbourne to compete in the Olympics. Since he was no longer an amateur, which was a prerequisite at the time for participating in the Olympics, he was in a bind. Cleverly, he ended up convincing the authorities with a nice spin, specifying that he would only be joining the NBA courts much later. A good initiative, since the American team, supercharged with adrenaline, went on to win gold in Australia.

As expected, the rookie didn't join the club until December 1956. Under the spell of their young teammate, the Celts felt like they'd grown wings. "Bill was more than just an exceptional player," said point guard Bob Cousy. "He didn't have the fundamentals of a Chamberlain or, later, an Abdul-Jabbar, but he played with such intensity that it became contagious." The Celtics' defense became relentless.

The 1957 NBA final against the St. Louis Hawks is remembered for the decisive Game 7. During the game, Bill Russell saved the Massachusetts starting five from disaster with a desperate comeback against Jack Coleman, who was about to sound the death knell for Boston. After two overtimes, the Celts

ON THIS DAY . . .

AUGUST 28, 1965

On August 28, 1965, Bill Russell signed a contract extension with the Boston Celtics, becoming the NBA's highest-paid player, with a salary of $100,001 per year . . . $1 more than that of a certain Wilt Chamberlain! The competition between the two men reached a climax, it even came to bank accounts, and the public became fascinated by the duel between the tenors of US basketball. It was more a staged event than a real arm-wrestling match, as the two men would admit many years later.

snatched victory (125–123). In early 1960, Wilt Chamberlain joined the Philadelphia Warriors, but the Celtics continued their dominance and, in Game 2 of the final, Bill Russell single-handedly pulled off 40 rebounds.

At the end of the 1964 season, the "Father of Defense" actually finished top rebounder ahead of Wilt Chamberlain! And the Celtics became the first franchise in American professional sports to win a sixth consecutive title. With the departure of his mentor Red Auerbach in 1966, Bill Russell took over on the bench and, in his role as player-coach, kept the group at the highest level. Marked by the political situation in the US, particularly after the assassinations of Martin Luther King Jr. and John F. Kennedy, Bill Russell took the blow hard. Basketball was no longer his priority, and the results were showing on the court.

On May 5, 1969, after another triumph, he tiptoed off the stage – without telling anyone. The Celtics, taken by surprise, had made no plans to recruit a new center. Three years later, Russell refused to take part in a ceremony in his honor, during which Boston withdrew its legendary number 6 from the squad. In 2009, he accepted public honors when the NBA decided that the MVP title would henceforth be known as the Bill Russell Trophy. "It's a source of pride to know that my name will be associated with this award for a long time to come," he said.

Bill Russell in action against the Cincinnati Royals in Cincinnati, January 1, 1970.

SERBIA

Predrag STOJAKOVIĆ

BORN ON: 9 June 1977

IN: Požega, Croatia

HEIGHT: 6'10" (2.08 m)

POSITION: Forward

PROFESSIONAL CAREER: PAOK Thessaloniki; Sacramento Kings; Indiana Pacers; New Orleans Hornets; Toronto Raptors; Dallas Mavericks

ACHIEVEMENTS: 1 World Championship title (2002); 1 Euro Championship title (2001); 1 NBA Championship title (2011)

Russell Westbrook of the Oklahoma City Thunder tries to block Peja Stojaković (16) during the NBA Western Conference Finals in Oklahoma City on May 23, 2011.

What do Pau Gasol, Toni Kukoč, and Predrag Stojaković all have in common? These three international basketball stars are the only ones to have achieved the sensational triple: World Champion–European Champion–NBA title! After winning gold at the Euro 2001 in Turkey – where he was voted MVP of the tournament – Predrag "Peja" Stojaković repeated the feat the following year at the World Championships in Indianapolis. In the quarterfinals, he pulled off a stunning upset, eliminating the United States on their home turf (81–78), before giving Argentina no chance in the final (84–77)!

ON THIS DAY . . .

NOVEMBER 15, 2006. "Peja on fire!" On November 14, 2006, in a memorable victory over the Charlotte Bobcats, Predrag Stojaković became the first player in NBA history to score the first 20 points for his New Orleans Hornets team. The following day, the local press ran the headline "Stojaković 20 – Charlotte 17" to illustrate this impressive solo display. Due to Hurricane Katrina, the game was relocated to Oklahoma City. But that didn't faze Peja, who scored a total of 42 points that day, winning 94–85.

THE SERBIAN SNIPER

With 13,647 points scored in the NBA throughout his career, Predrag Stojaković ranks 25th in three-point scoring in the NBA, with a total of 1,760 baskets from beyond the arc out of 4,392 attempts, representing a success rate of over 40 percent in this difficult skill. In fact, Predrag claimed the competition title twice (2002 and 2003) at the All-Star Game. With surgical precision, Peja was renowned for his unpredictability when attempting shots from behind the arc, in what are known as "long twos," from more than 16 feet away from the hoop.

Considered one of the most adept outside shooters, Peja found an improbable angle even when he was in a crazy position, millimeters from the edge of the court, behind the backboard! He had an unconventional shooting technique, and many commentators thought of him as a disjointed puppet. "When Peja takes a shot, he looks like a drunk man about to fall over," said ESPN journalist Frank Hughes. "His arms and legs fly everywhere!"

Trained by Red Star Belgrade during his teenage years, Peja was not yet of legal age when he joined the Greek league. His parents, Branka and Miodrag, Serbian by birth but caught up in the war in the former Yugoslavia, agreed to let Peja live out his passion for basketball at PAOK Thessaloniki. "From the age of 14, I started practicing three-point shooting twice a day," he said. My coach insisted that I take between 500 and 800 shots a day. On the other hand, he never tried to modify my body language."

A DIAMOND IN THE ROUGH

When he turned 18, Peja also obtained Greek nationality. Europe was sniffing around, but his fledgling reputation spread across the Atlantic, and he caught the eye of Byron Scott, his future coach at the New Orleans Hornets. However, during the 1998 American draft, it was the Sacramento Kings who got their hands on him. In the California squad, captain Vlade Divac took the rookie under his wing and, despite the presence of strong personalities such as Chris Robinson, Tariq Abdul-Wahad, and Jason Williams, Peja quickly made his mark.

His 2003–2004 season was phenomenal. Sacramento had a growing fan base, drawn by the consistent quality of its play and its lyrical flights of fancy. The team was formidable on the court, but its mental strength in crunch time was considered shaky, and when the playoffs rolled around, the Kings were knocked off their throne.

After eight seasons with the Kings, Predrag set himself a new challenge, joining the Indiana Pacers in January 2006. That lasted just six months, before a switch to the New Orleans Hornets, with a five-year, $64 million contract. Unfortunately, the Serbian forward's first season with the Hornets was marred by repeated injuries and, despite scoring 42 points against the Charlotte Bobcats, his debut left a feeling of unfulfilled potential. The following year, Peja redeemed himself, making 77 appearances as a first-team regular. And it was no coincidence that, for the first time in their history, the Hornets won 56 games in a single season.

Despite Peja's efforts, the Hornets still missed out in the final stages of the playoffs. But the three-point sniper was determined to make his mark on the NBA. In November 2010, he opted for the Toronto Raptors, but three months later, after playing only two games, he was released from his contract. Peja missed 26 games with a nasty left knee injury. In January 2011, he was off to the Dallas Mavericks.

A FIRST ATTEMPT – AND A TOTAL TRIUMPH!

In the NBA Finals against the Heat, averaging over 20 points per game on two occasions, Peja led the Dallas Mavericks to its first-ever NBA title. On June 12, 2011, the Texans pulled off a 105–95 victory to clinch the title (4–2). After this remarkable achievement, Stojaković bowed out in glory. One of the all-time greats, Peja took his final bow at the peak of a career rich in achievements.

DID YOU KNOW?

In a moving ceremony in December 2014 at the brand-new, 17,500-seat Golden 1 Center, the Sacramento Kings celebrated Predrag Stojaković. During the evening, the Californian club's owner, Vivek Ranadivé, paid tribute to him: "Peja helped put Sacramento on the world map." Stojaković then took the microphone to say that he was "proud of what we have built and the connection we have established with the fans." His famous number 16 was then retired from the team.

Predrag Stojaković (16) during the Dallas Mavericks-Los Angeles Lakers NBA Western Conference semifinal game at Crypto.com Arena in Los Angeles, May 4, 2011.

UNITED STATES

Isiah

THOMAS

BORN ON: 30 April 30 1961

IN: Chicago

HEIGHT: 6'1" (1.85 m)

POSITION: Point Guard

PROFESSIONAL CAREER: Detroit Pistons

ACHIEVEMENTS: 2 NBA championship titles (1989, 1990); 1 NBA Finals MVP title (1990); 1 NBA Citizenship Award (1987)

Detroit Pistons' Isiah Thomas (11) charges past Boston Celtics' Danny Ainge (44) on February 28, 1988.

Sometimes considered Magic Johnson 2.0, Isiah Thomas is also forever linked to his role as leader of the Detroit "Bad Boys," a franchise that terrorized and dominated the league at the turn of the 1980s and 1990s. A man of many contradictions, the two-time NBA winner overcame a difficult childhood and constant adversity to become one of the greatest point guards ever.

DID YOU KNOW?

In December 2024, Isiah Thomas, now a sports commentator, revealed that he was suffering from Bell's palsy. This condition, diagnosed earlier in 2024, causes facial paralysis and a distorted smile, and can affect a person's ability to open their eyes. Normally, this paralysis isn't permanent, but some fans were nevertheless alarmed to see their idol physically affected.

FROM THE STREETS TO THE LARRY O'BRIEN TROPHY

Growing up in Chicago's poorest neighborhoods, Isiah Thomas might never have become an NBA star or legend. The youngest of nine siblings, he grew up without a father, while his mother juggled jobs to support the family. It was Isiah's brother Henry who trained him and pushed him into basketball, a real lifeline for a kid destined for the streets. Isiah soon enrolled in a private school where he found a more stable environment and was able to develop as a player. In his junior year, he led St. Joseph to the finals, and by the end of high school he would be considered one of the top prospects for the college courts. In 1979 he was recruited to play for the Indiana Hoosiers, champions three times in their history. Thomas was instrumental in securing the fourth victory under the legendary Bob Knight, who had been coaching Indiana for 29 years. Against James Worthy's North Carolina (No. 1 in the 1982 draft), Thomas scored 23 points and won the title of Most Outstanding Player. A few months later, he headed to the NBA as the second pick in the draft. And the point guard didn't have far to go, landing in Detroit, Michigan.

At the Pistons, "Zeke" was tasked with bringing back to the playoffs a franchise that hadn't known the joys of the postseason for four seasons. It would take them three more seasons to qualify for the next nine, led by their point guard. However, it wasn't long before Thomas began to dominate the NBA courts. An All-Star in his very first season, he returned to the game's biggest stage for 12 years, winning two All-Star Game MVP awards, and laying the foundations for his future success. It took the Pistons two seasons to get back to winning ways, but they remained in the top six of the Eastern Conference until 1992–1993. It was here that Thomas achieved his first feats, such

as forcing overtime in the first round of the 1984 playoffs against the Knicks, scoring 16 points in 94 seconds! He was skilled in all areas of the game – passing, shooting, creating, scoring, and defense.

Along with his teammates Joe Dumars, Dennis Rodman, and Bill Laimbeer, he embodied the spirit of the Detroit Bad Boys, a team that became a legend, adored as much as it was hated.

Detroit Pistons' Isiah Thomas (11) charges past Boston Celtics' Danny Ainge (44) on February 28, 1988.

Known for their ultra-physical, violent play, often bordering on excessive, the Pistons relied on their skills but also on their determination to rattle their opponents. Under Chuck Daly, the head coach who led Detroit to the Conference Finals between 1987 and 1991, the entire franchise became one of the best in the country, reaching its peak between 1988 and 1990 with three consecutive finals appearances.

In 1988, the Pistons finished the regular season in second place in the East, while Thomas's statistics declined slightly. After knocking out the top-seeded Celtics, the Bad Boys faced the defending champions, the Lakers, for the title. Leading 3–2 going into Game 6, the Michigan men were

Isiah Thomas (11) scores over Boston Celtics' Dennis Johnson (3) and Jim Paxton (4) during the NBA Semifinals game in Detroit, Michigan, in 1988.

ON THIS DAY . . .

In the early 1990s, the Pistons and their Bad Boys weren't exactly popular in the NBA, to say the least. Accused of playing dirty, they were irritating and frustrating. Isiah Thomas was the symbol of this team, and Karl Malone knew it. So, one evening in December 1991, during a Utah-Detroit game, the center sent a nasty elbow to the point guard as he was driving to the hoop. The latter required 40 stitches around his eye, a testimony to the violence of the blow.

within reach of their first championship ring. In the third quarter, Thomas was on fire with 14 straight points but suffered a serious ankle injury. Just when fans thought his game was over, he came back before the final quarter, galvanized by the prospect of a championship. He scored 11 more points to finish the third quarter with an NBA record of 25 points! With 43 points, 8 assists, and 6 steals, he did everything in his power to win his first ring, but the referees got in the way. They called an imaginary foul on Bill Laimbeer, and Kareem-Abdul Jabbar scored two free throws to force Game 7, which the Lakers won easily. The dream seemed to be over. However, the following year, Thomas and his teammates returned to the finals – and the Lakers.

Better and more mature, the Pistons made short work of the Californians, winning 4–0. Isiah was finally a champion. This first title would quickly be followed by another the next year against Portland. It was a 4–1 victory without breaking a sweat, after beating Jordan's Bulls in the conference finals. This time, the MVP title was Zeke's for the taking. With his 27.6 points, 7 assists, and 5.2 rebounds, he was simply out of this world. In a sign of a different era, he only took 16 three-point shots over the five games, making 11 of them. The rest of his career was less impressive: injured in his Achilles tendon at the end of the 1994 season, the point guard decided to hang up his worn-out sneakers. The best player in Pistons history, his number 11 jersey was retired in 1996, and he was inducted into the Hall of Fame in 2000.

UNITED STATES

Klay THOMPSON

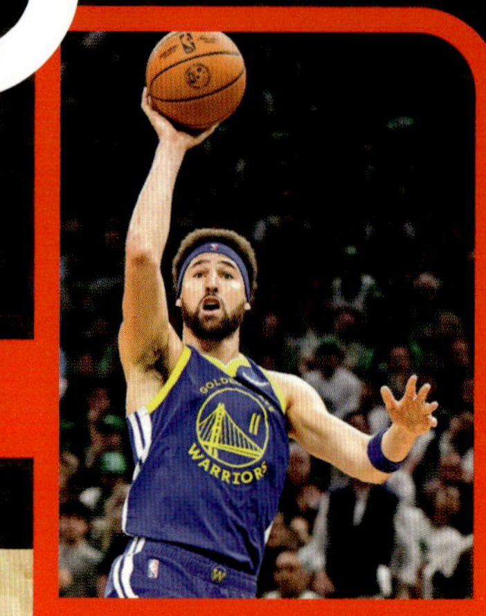

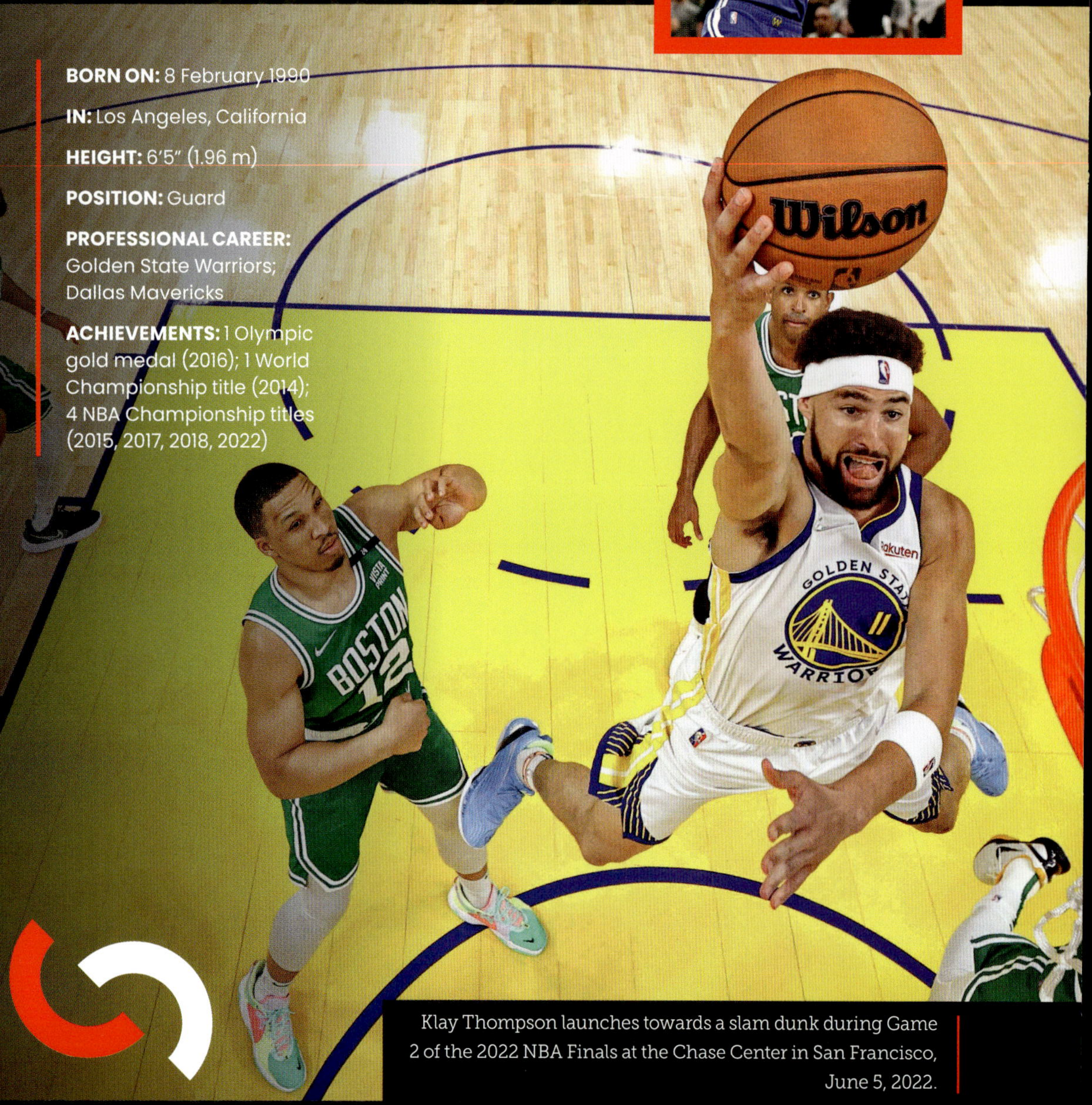

BORN ON: 8 February 1990

IN: Los Angeles, California

HEIGHT: 6'5" (1.96 m)

POSITION: Guard

PROFESSIONAL CAREER: Golden State Warriors; Dallas Mavericks

ACHIEVEMENTS: 1 Olympic gold medal (2016); 1 World Championship title (2014); 4 NBA Championship titles (2015, 2017, 2018, 2022)

Klay Thompson launches towards a slam dunk during Game 2 of the 2022 NBA Finals at the Chase Center in San Francisco, June 5, 2022.

Renowned for his infernal three-point shooting, Klay Alexander Thompson has earned his spurs in the NBA. Recognized as one of the league's best shooters of all time, thanks to his fluidity of movement, the Californian guard possesses a silky shot. The thing is, his flair – and almost arrogant success – from long range is a double-edged sword. Some commentators feel that he should be confined to this role, and others even doubt his ability to keep the ball alive. Even Stephen Curry is offended by this: "His playmaking ability is underrated."

RAISED ON BASKETBALL

Klay's father Mychal, originally from the Bahamas, was the center for the Los Angeles Lakers, with whom he won the title in 1987 and 1988, alongside Kareem Abdul-Jabbar and Magic Johnson. From Klay's first steps on the courts at Santa Margarita Catholic High School, the heir quickly became a true technical leader. But it was, of course, at college, with the Washington State Cougars, that "the Electrician" – named for his ability to send volts down the court – really came into his own. As the top scorer and best interceptor on his team, the young Klay racked up some incredible statistics.

During the 2011 summer draft, Klay's versatility and skill in all positions attracted big-name franchises. However, doubts remained about his ability to compete at the highest level. He was only ranked 11th on the Warriors' list, but they signed him anyway. Under coach Mark Jackson, the rookie got off to a tentative start. After a lackluster performance in one match, he surprised all his teammates – he was so angry that he left the arena without even stopping at the locker room showers, rushing home in his uniform!

A STRONG CHARACTER

Klay Thompson was champing at the bit, but he knew that when his chance came, he couldn't let it slip away. Monta Ellis's departure to Milwaukee opened up that opportunity, and he jumped at it. In the 2012–2013 season, Klay made 82 appearances in the regular season alone. The Thompson-Curry duo became a force to be

ON THIS DAY . . .

OCTOBER 29, 2018

Made for the record books: On October 29, 2018, against the Chicago Bulls (in a 149–124 victory for Golden State), Klay Thompson scored 14 three-pointers in just 27 minutes. The Warriors guard then surpassed his teammate Stephen Curry, the record-holder until then, by one shot. Not to be outdone, Thompson also equaled the performance of Chandler Parsons, the Atlanta Hawks forward, by sinking an impressive 10 three-pointers in a row, without missing a single attempt.

reckoned with in the backcourt. The two teammates were nicknamed the "Splash Brothers" in reference to the sound the ball made when it grazed the rim. Not yet a regular, Klay Thompson was nevertheless the most-used player in the following year. Curry made a staggering 261 three-pointers, while Thompson made 223!

Coach Mark Johnson campaigned for his guard. "Klay defends better, performs better on pick-and-rolls, and makes better decisions. What he does on both sides of the court puts him in a class of his own." Rumors of a move to Minnesota were leaked to the sports press, but new coach Steve Kerr was keen to keep his star player, and Klay finally agreed to a four-year contract extension with a $70 million bonus.

At the end of 2014, Klay put in a string of hard-fought performances, particularly in terms of points: 41 against the Los Angeles Lakers, then 52 against the Sacramento Kings. "Klay will still be able to shoot, even when he's 75," joked Steve Kerr, who was clearly impressed. In January 2015, Thompson scored the most points ever in a single quarter of an NBA game, with 37 against the Kings. The season was capped by an absolute triumph in the playoffs, after the final victory over LeBron James' Cleveland Cavaliers (4–2).

ALWAYS READY!

In February 2016, during the All-Star Game, Klay Thompson challenged his own teammate Stephen Curry in the three-point contest. In front of a crowd in a frenzy over this spectacular duel between the Splash Brothers, Klay came out on top. A few weeks later, things were looking much less rosy. Curry was injured and a weakened Golden State lost its crown to the resurgent Cavaliers. But it was only a temporary setback. Six months later, Thompson scored 60 points in just 29 minutes against the Indiana Pacers, setting a new NBA record. At the end of the season, the Warriors reclaimed the title from Cleveland with a playoff record of 16 wins and just one defeat.

In June 2019, as they prepared to face the Toronto Raptors in the finals, the worst happened. First, Curry was suffering from a nasty foot sprain. And then, in Game 6

From left to right: Draymond Green (23), Klay Thompson (11), and Stephen Curry (30) celebrate their victory over the Boston Celtics in Game 6 of the NBA Finals 2022 at the TD Garden in Boston, June 16, 2022.

DID YOU KNOW?

Known for his laid-back attitude, Klay Thompson still managed to surprise the Warriors' management. During the initial negotiations for his contract, the young guard suddenly stood up and said: "Guys, I've got to go home, I have to feed Rocco!" Rocco was his bulldog. After a Conference semifinal, the Californian even went into the shower with his dog. Brazilian player Anderson Varejão summed it up: "You don't see that anywhere in the NBA, except with Klay Thompson!"

against the Raptors, disaster struck when Thompson's left knee gave way. The verdict: a torn anterior cruciate ligament, requiring surgery.

The 2020–2021 season would be just as bleak, as Thompson followed up with a ruptured Achilles tendon in his right foot! After 30 months out of action on the courts, Klay returned and, thanks to 41 points scored against the New Orleans Pelicans, he said: "After what I've been through, I'll never take a 40-plus point game lightly again!" A true specialist in delivering sparks, both on and off the court – always catching you off guard.

UNITED STATES

Russell

WESTBROOK

BORN ON: 12 November 1988

IN: Long Beach, California

HEIGHT: 6'4" (1.93 m)

POSITION: Guard

PROFESSIONAL CAREER: Oklahoma City Thunder; Houston Rockets; Washington Wizards; Los Angeles Lakers; Los Angeles Clippers; Denver Nuggets

ACHIEVEMENTS: 1 Olympic gold medal (2012); 1 World Championship title (2010); 1 NBA regular season MVP title (2017)

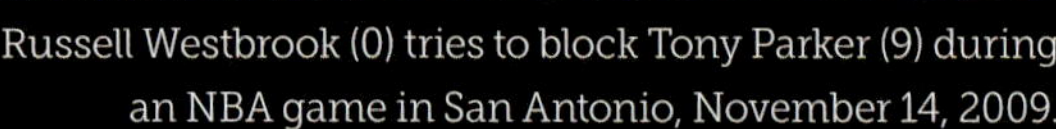

Russell Westbrook (0) tries to block Tony Parker (9) during an NBA game in San Antonio, November 14, 2009.

Russell Westbrook is the Swiss army knife of American basketball. In fact, his nickname, "Mister Triple-Double," is well-deserved. The Californian point guard is the first player in NBA history to have achieved a triple-double in four consecutive seasons, based on his statistics for successful shots, assists, and rebounds. A perfect athlete with above-average power, he knows how to weave his way perfectly between defenders and demonstrate an unparalleled sense of teamwork.

ON THIS DAY . . .

FEBRUARY 14, 2019
Among his dizzying array of statistics, Russell Westbrook can mark February 14, 2019, with a white cross. He entered the annals of American basketball history that evening – the Oklahoma City point guard broke the record for consecutive triple-doubles (11 in total), surpassing the legendary Wilt Chamberlain, who had held the record since 1968. Westbrook also shattered the record for points scored for a single franchise (18,207).

THE RARE PEARL

Surprisingly, the future Beastbrook didn't look like a beast when he was a teenager, due to late growth. Rather puny and unable to dunk, the little genius used steps to perfect his physical bulk. "I worked a lot on my footwork, with squats and going up and down stairs," he recalled. He grew up in the southern suburbs of Los Angeles, trained by his father on the Hawthorne neighborhood playgrounds. In his final year at Leuzinger High School, Russell began to grow like bamboo and, at the last minute, got a scholarship to the University of California, Los Angeles.

A starter in his second season with the Bruins, Russell was particularly sought after by several NBA franchises looking for the right player. It was a toss-up between the SuperSonics and the Thunder, but he ended up in Oklahoma City where he quickly made his mark, forming a fiery trio with Kevin Durant and Jeff Green. He chose the surprising number zero on his jersey. "This is not just any number," said Russell Westbrook. "You take it when you've been through tough times and you're looking for a fresh start."

The crowd rubbed their eyes in disbelief as they watched this little wonder on springs (who at the time was less than 6 feet tall) dunk the ball. On March 2, 2009, Russell scored his first triple-double, becoming the youngest to do so since LeBron James. The following season, he discovered the playoffs, but the eventual winners, the Los Angeles Lakers, didn't give an inch. Nevertheless, his rebounding performances impressed everyone. Skeptics suspected that the new Thunderbolt was stealing loose balls from his better-positioned teammates to pad his stats! This was a rather restrictive view, given that Westbrook, always quick to

sidestep the spotlight, had a complete skill set in all areas of the game.

In 2011, "Beastbrook" withstood the pressure of a Game 7 playoff match, this time against the Memphis Grizzlies, where he became only the fifth player to achieve a triple-double in such a decisive game, after Jerry West (1969), Larry Bird (1984), James Worthy (1988), and Scottie Pippen (1992). Not too shabby! The following season, he further refined his game. His incredible chemistry with Kevin Durant was a delight to watch. When the playoffs arrived, however, a meniscus injury meant surgery. He underwent further surgery on his right knee the following summer and had to wait until November 2013 to return to the court. The relief was short-lived – further surgeries ruled him out of the All-Star Game.

In front of ecstatic fans in March 2014, the triple-double machine achieved his ninth triple-double (13 points, 10 rebounds, 14 assists) in just 20 minutes. It was the second-fastest triple-double in NBA history!

BACK TO THE TOP

Everything would have been fine for Oklahoma City if the two stars, Russell Westbrook and Kevin Durant, hadn't injured their hand and foot respectively. The Thunder then lost 12 games in a row. The return of the infernal duo to the Paycom Center revived the franchise.

In April 2015, Russell Westbrook made headlines in the local sports press with his 54 points – a personal best – against the Indiana Pacers. At the 2016 All-Star Game, Beastbrook was voted MVP for the second year running. This was a first since Bob Pettit, power forward for the St. Louis Hawks, in 1958 and 1959!

The Thunder also benefited from the return of a pumped-up Kevin Durant, meaning Russell Westbrook was no longer alone. However, it was the end of an era with Kevin Durant's departure in the summer to the Golden State Warriors. Rumors of exile for the Thunder's number zero haunted Oklahoma pubs but the Californian lightning bolt remained loyal, extending his contract by three years. MVP of the 2016–2017 season, he broke the all-time record for triple-doubles

Russell Westbrook during the Washington Wizards-Charlotte Hornets game at Capital One Arena in Washington, DC, on May 16, 2021.

DID YOU KNOW?

During warm-ups between the Lakers and the Milwaukee Bucks in November 2021, Russell Westbrook donned a jersey emblazoned with the name of Julius Jones, who was languishing on death row in an Oklahoma jail cell. Despite lingering doubts about the investigation, Jones had been sentenced to death and was awaiting his execution, still proclaiming his innocence. The next day, Governor Kevin Stitt, under pressure from prominent figures such as the Californian point guard, commuted Julius Jones's sentence to life imprisonment a few hours before his scheduled execution.

(42 in total) in a single season, surpassing the legendary Kareem Abdul-Jabbar.

In July 2019, after eleven seasons with the Thunder, Russell Westbrook signed with the Houston Rockets. After years of stability, things became much more turbulent for the brilliant point guard, who, a year and a half later, joined the Washington Wizards, even giving up his favorite number for a less original 4. Back to square one in the summer of 2021, Westbrook settled in Los Angeles, joining the Lakers, then went on to the Clippers. After a 2024 move to the Denver Nuggets, in 2025 he declined his option to extend his contract for another year.

Wilt Chamberlain scored a total of 31,419 points, averaging 30.1 per game throughout 1,045 games, in a career that lasted 16 years. He was the highest scorer in the NBA for seven consecutive years.

1962

Wilt Chamberlain's unbeatable scoring record

On March 2, 1962, the Philadelphia Warriors center broke his own NBA single-game scoring record with 100 points against the New York Knicks. A legendary feat that no one has come close to matching it in the 60 years since.

A HISTORIC MOMENT

The photo has endured through the years, immortalizing that historic moment. In this shot, Wilt Chamberlain is sitting on the ground, a white jersey draped over his shoulders, smiling and sporting a neatly trimmed moustache. In his hands, Chamberlain proudly displays a piece of paper on which the number 100 has been scribbled by hand. It is proof that those involved in the game already knew that the performance would go down in basketball history. The photo is the only visual record of the event, with a radio recording but no video footage.

Philadelphia hosted the New York franchise, last on the ladder in the Eastern Conference, in a meaningless game with only five regular season games remaining. In fact, only 4,124 spectators were in the 7,200-capacity Hershey Sports Arena, outside Philadelphia. They didn't know it yet, but they would be the privileged few to witness one of the most legendary feats in the history of basketball.

Thanks to his height (7 foot 1; 2.16 m) and agility, Wilt Chamberlain dominated his direct rivals in the center position all season long. The Philadelphia native was the league's leading scorer in his first two NBA seasons and had an even more impressive third season on offense. Less than three months earlier, on December 8, 1961, he had already set the record for most points scored in a single game, scoring 78 in a 151–147 loss to the Los Angeles Lakers after three overtimes. His opponent that night, and former record holder with 71 points, Elgin Baylor, said, "One day, this guy's going to score 100 points."

From the very first minutes of March 2, 1962, Chamberlain continued his crazy streak of three consecutive games with more than 60 points (67, 65, and 61). Facing the Knicks,

"Wilt the Stilt" (his nickname due to his long legs) started the game as usual, no hint of the performance he would deliver by the end of the evening.

With 23 points in the first quarter, followed by 18 in the second, Chamberlain had 41 at half-time, a score he was used to at that point in the game. But things really got going in the second half. In the third quarter, he scored a further 28 points to take his total to 69 with one final quarter still to play.

A RECORD THAT SEEMED DESTINED TO STAND FOREVER

In the final quarter, with just over 10 minutes remaining, the center scored his 79th point, already surpassing his career record. Everything changed in an instant, and the 4,124 spectators wanted only one thing – to see him break the record for eternity. "Give the ball to Wilt!" chanted the crowd. The Warriors listened to their fans and fed their teammate the ball.

The score climbed, but the Knicks didn't want to be victims of Wilt Chamberlain's record. Knowing the Warrior's difficulties with free throws, they decided to foul him repeatedly to send him to the line. Wilt, who had a modest 51.1 percent career free throw success rate, enjoyed incredible accuracy that day, converting 28 of the 32 free throws he attempted, for an 87.5 percent success rate.

It was thanks to two signature dunks that he finally reached the iconic 100-point mark. "I always thought it was inevitable that he would do it. But when he did, I stopped – I couldn't believe it," exclaimed his coach, Frank McGuire. The crowd poured onto the court to congratulate their player with 46 seconds left in the game. He remained convinced for a long time that the final seconds of the game were not played, before realizing years later that they had indeed, with a victory for his team (169–147).

During this game, Wilt Chamberlain broke a total of 10 records, some of which still stand today: the record for points scored in a half (59), the number of shots made (36) and attempted (63), and the number of shots made (22) and attempted (37) in a half. Yet the star didn't rest on his laurels. "It doesn't mean anything if we don't win the title," he said.

Unfortunately, the Philadelphia Warriors fell in the conference final to the eventual NBA champions, the Boston Celtics (4 games to 3). Chamberlain still won two NBA titles in his career – with the Philadelphia Sixers in 1967 (formerly the Syracuse Nationals) and with the Los Angeles Lakers in 1972.

The four-time MVP (1960, 1966, 1967, and 1968) died on October 12, 1999, in Bel Air, California, and his record has never been challenged. Kobe Bryant is the only one to have come close. On January 22, 2006, the Lakers guard scored 81 points against the Toronto Raptors.

American basketball legend Wilt Chamberlain (13) playing for the Philadelphia Warriors in 1960.

PHILA
13

Michael Jordan playing for the USA Team (9) at the 1992 Olympic Summer Games in Barcelona

1992

The Dream Team on top of Mount Olympus

Featuring Michael Jordan, Larry Bird, and Magic Johnson, the US team defeated Croatia on August 8, 1992, to win the gold medal at the Barcelona Olympics thanks to a unique combination of talent.

"You'll see more professional teams at the Olympics, but I don't think you'll see another team like this one. It was a great team." The words of Chuck Daly, coach of the US national team at the 1992 Barcelona Olympics, are hard to argue with given the wealth of talent that made up Team USA at the time. Michael Jordan, Larry Bird, Magic Johnson, Charles Barkley, David Robinson, Patrick Ewing, Scottie Pippen, Clyde Drexler, Karl Malone, John Stockton, Chris Mullin, and Christian Laettner – never has a team looked so strong in the history of basketball.

A TEAM OF ROCK STARS

Bringing together all these extraordinary talents was made possible by a decision by the International Olympic Committee and FIBA (the International Basketball Federation) in 1989 to allow professional players from the NBA to participate in the Games. Previously, Team USA was made up exclusively of college players such as Michael Jordan, Chris Mullin, and Patrick Ewing, who had already won gold in Los Angeles in 1984.

For the 1992 Olympics, the first eleven names were quickly put down on paper, and most of these players were at the peak of their NBA careers. The selection committee finally decided to add a player from the NCAA, the university championship. Two-time college champion Christian Laettner was chosen over Shaquille O'Neal, the number one pick in the 1992 NBA draft.

The team soon earned the nickname "Dream Team" from journalists around the world. More than just an adjective, it became the team's quasi-official name. "I felt like I was bringing together the Beatles and Elvis Presley," summed up coach Chuck Daly. "Traveling with the Dream Team was like traveling with 12 rock stars. That's the only thing I can compare them to."

Proof of their immense fame, the Dream Team did not stay in the Olympic Village for security reasons. Chuck Daly's players occupied a hotel in the city, where fans gathered every day hoping to get a photo of their idols.

VICTIMS OF THE DREAM TEAM

Angola was the first team to suffer the wrath of the Americans (116–48). This was followed by straightforward group stage victories over Croatia (103–70), Germany (111–68), Brazil (127–83), and Spain (122–81). Puerto Rico (115–77) and Lithuania (127–76) offered little resistance in the quarterfinals and semifinals, respectively.

On August 8, 1992, in the final of the Olympic Games, the Dream Team faced Croatia, whom they had already beaten in the group phase. World champions and two-time European champions before the Barcelona Games, Yugoslavia seemed to be the only team capable of taking on the United States. However, Yugoslavia was being torn apart by a war in 1992. Croatia was ultimately the only team to represent the country.

Thanks to the talent of Toni Kukoč (16 points), Dražen Petrović (24 points), and Dino Radja (23 points), Croatia had the luxury of leading at the end of the first quarter (25–23). Only Spain had managed to lead the competition ahead of Team USA.

The US then took the lead by shutting down Toni Kukoč.

On offense, Michael Jordan once again did the job. He finished as his team's top scorer with 22 points, while six of his teammates scored more than 10 points: Charles Barkley (17 points), Patrick Ewing (15 points), Scottie Pippen (12 points), Chris Mullin (11 points), Magic Johnson (11 points), and Clyde Drexler (10 points).

In the end, the Dream Team won by 32 points (117–85), the smallest margin of victory during the competition. In doing so, they secured a 10th Olympic title for Team USA, the first since 1984.

The Dream Team on the podium at the 1992 Olympic Games in Barcelona.

"We were able to do what everyone expected of us," said Michael Jordan. "Today, we can once again be proud of our basketball program."

AN IMMENSE LEGACY

This dream team was inducted into the Basketball Hall of Fame in 2010 and the FIBA Hall of Fame in 2017. Only one other team has ever come close to such a collection of talent. At the London 2012 Games, Team USA brought together Kobe Bryant, LeBron James, Carmelo Anthony, Kevin Durant, Chris Paul, and James Harden. Kobe Bryant and LeBron James had the misfortune to declare that they would have beaten the Dream Team. Larry Bird responded with a sense of humor: "They would probably beat us. I haven't played in 20 years and we're old now."

Magic Johnson playing for the LA Lakers (13) against the Cleveland Cavaliers during the NBA Pacific Division basketball game on January 11, 1991 in Inglewood, Los Angeles. The Lakers won the game 105–93.

1992

Magic Johnson smiles again

A few weeks after the announcement of his illness, in February 1992, the Lakers point guard was invited to take part in his 12th All-Star Game in Orlando. Though out of competitive rhythm, he was voted MVP at the end of an emotional evening.

While the score had long since been settled, with the Western Conference's crushing 153–113 defeat of its East Coast rivals, time seemed to stand still with 14 seconds remaining. On the star-studded court, this All-Star Game, extraordinary in more ways than one, came to a premature end, as all the NBA's greatest players wanted to honor Earvin "Magic" Johnson, who, at the age of 32, had just gone through a terrible period of anxiety.

A TRAUMATIC SHOCK

Four months earlier, doctors had diagnosed him with HIV, and this exceptional champion, along with a whole country and fans around the world, was in shock.

Since the medical announcement, followed by his battle with the disease and the psychological aspect that goes with it, Magic Johnson hadn't touched a ball, and his season had been unremarkable. Moreover, when he was selected for the event, there were doubts about the performance of a player who had been sidelined by circumstances beyond his control. Others, concerned about this still little-known virus, which stirred up many disturbing misconceptions, were afraid of coming into contact with Magic, who was almost considered a pariah. Anticipating these concerns, Johnson sought to reassure them: "The doctors have assured me that there's no chance of me passing it on to anyone on the court. So, there's no risk." The five-time NBA champion pulled out all the stops to be ready on the big day. With the ambiguity now cleared up, the tribute could begin.

BIG-NIGHT CROWDS AT ORLANDO

On February 9, 1992, nearly 15,000 fans took to the seats in the glittering, rhinestone-clad Orlando Arena. When the announcer called his name with a long bellow of "Earvin Maaaaaaagic Jooooooooohnson!" a rapturous ovation shook the walls of the red-hot Florida arena.

It echoed loudly in the aisles and in people's hearts. To break down all prejudices, Isiah Thomas gave the hero of the day a warm embrace. Perfect for getting back into the swing of things, with that radiant smile that fans had missed so much. One after another, Chris Mullin, Larry Bird, Michael Jordan, Dennis Rodman, Scottie Pippen, Hakeem Olajuwon, and even Charles Barkley came to pay tribute to the living legend.

Sixty-five seconds into the game, the Michigan native, more tense because of the buzz around him than because of what was at stake, missed his first shot, but recovered on the rebound before drawing a foul. He scored his first two points of the evening from free throws. As the game went on, Magic found his energy and completely let loose. He set the arena alight in the final quarter, while the on-air reporters shouted themselves hoarse.

The final moments reached their climax when number 32, with his pressing, caused Isiah Thomas to lose his cool, resulting in an unlikely airball at the very end of the game. And then there was that block on Michael Jordan, who rarely looked so taken aback as he did at that precise moment. The absolute legend completed his performance with three consecutive three-pointers, including the last shot of the game. With 29 minutes played in this emotional comeback, Magic Johnson left the court relieved after an unforgettable gala evening: "It went exactly the way I wanted it to. I'm going to cherish this moment for the rest of my life!"

To complete the celebration, the Lakers' point guard was named MVP of this historic All-Star Game. "It was a kind of therapy to keep me going in life," said the divine Earvin "Magic" Johnson, who played on until the Barcelona Olympics, where, with an outstanding Dream Team, won a gold medal worth all the treatment in the world.

Earvin "Magic" Johnson in action.

LAKERS
32

Michael Jordan leans on his teammate Scottie Pippen to leave the court.

1997

The flu game – Michael Jordan, stronger than the flu

On June 11, 1997, Michael Jordan put in a fantastic performance in Game 5 of the NBA Finals against the Utah Jazz, despite being bedridden just a few hours earlier by a violent bout of flu or food poisoning.

Without even winning a title or breaking a record, Michael Jordan succeeded in making history – further proof, if any were needed, of the imprint left by the man many consider to be the sport's GOAT (Greatest Of All Time).

SHOWDOWN AT THE TOP

Michael Jordan's Chicago Bulls were facing the Utah Jazz in the NBA Finals, hoping to retain their title from the previous season, the fourth of Jordan's career. The game was crucial, a decisive turning point in this best-of-seven series, as the two franchises were tied at two wins apiece.

However, the day before the game at the Delta Center in Salt Lake City, "His Airness," as he was nicknamed, woke up with a fever and feeling nauseous. He spent the next two days in bed with what appeared to be food poisoning. Or maybe even deliberate poisoning, according to Tim Grover, his fitness trainer at the time. "Everything was closed from 8.30 pm and there was no room service. Michael was hungry, so I found a local pizzeria that delivered," he recounted in 2020. "When I opened the door, there were five guys waiting outside to catch a glimpse of Michael. I said, 'I've got a bad feeling about this pizza, Mike.' He told me to get lost."

The day before the game, Michael Jordan didn't train. Nor did he train on the day itself. He was in a weak state; dehydrated, he had even lost a few pounds. But a few hours before the game, the Bulls guard left the hotel and made his way to the arena on his own. "At no point did I think he would be in uniform. I'd never seen him

like that," said teammate Scottie Pippen after the game.

Starting Game 5 despite his physical condition – MJ never starts on the bench – Michael Jordan was unable to stem his team's poor start: down 13 after one quarter and trailing by as many as 16 points in the second quarter (36–20).

FOREVER A LEGEND

The four-time NBA champion at the time regularly leaned forward, hands on his knees, exhausted. During every time-out, or the little time he spent off the court, he slumped on the bench. The player was sweating and still seemed feverish. But before the break, he managed to step up his aggression and his skill followed suit. With 21 points, he brought his team back into contention (53–49 for Utah).

When they returned from the locker room, Michael Jordan seemed once again affected by his flu-like symptoms. Struggling, he scored just two points in the third quarter and Utah thought they could take advantage. But they weren't counting on a legendary final quarter from the four-time MVP of the season (1988, 1991, 1992, and 1996, with a fifth and final MVP award in 1998).

With 11 points, he sparked a 10–0 run that gave his team a chance to win Game 5. In the final minute, he was awarded two free throws. He scored the first to level at 85–85 but missed the second. Fortunately, he grabbed his own rebound. At the end of this play, well served by Scottie Pippen, who was caught between two opponents, Michael Jordan sank the three-pointer that sealed the victory (88–85).

When the final buzzer went, Michael Jordan, with 38 points (including 15 in the final quarter), 7 rebounds, 5 assists, and 3 steals, collapsed exhausted into Scottie Pippen's arms. "He's the greatest, and everyone understood why tonight," said Pippen, admiring his leader's fierce competitive spirit.

"Given the circumstances, in such an important match, I have to admit that this is the greatest performance I've seen from Michael. Just standing there was hard for him, a truly heroic effort. One more in his legendary collection," said his coach, Phil Jackson. "It's probably the hardest thing I've ever done. If we'd lost, I'd have been devastated," said the hero of Match 5.

Two days later, back in Chicago, the Bulls won Game 6 (90–86) and the title in the process, thanks to another dazzling performance from MJ (39 points). He was voted MVP of the Finals, as he had been for his first four NBA titles.

Years later, rumors circulated that Jordan was not actually suffering from the flu or food poisoning, but from a late night of heavy drinking. Legendary nights are often shrouded in myth, where it's sometimes difficult to separate fact from fiction. Michael Jordan and the flu game are no exception.

A visibly debilitated Michael Jordan (23) competing against the Utah Jazz during the 1997 NBA finals.

BULLS
23

Michael Jordan holds the MVP trophy after the team's victory over the Utah Jazz. The Chicago Bulls won their sixth NBA title in Salt Lake City on June 14, 1998.

1998

Michael Jordan's last shot for the Bulls

On June 14, 1998, in what was meant to be the last game of his career, Michael Jordan made one last decisive shot for the Chicago Bulls to win his sixth and final NBA title.

LIKE A RENAISSANCE PAINTING

MJ, wearing a red Bulls jersey emblazoned with his iconic number 23, soared through the air. The ball had already left his hands and the clock above the basket showed 6.6 seconds left. Most of the players, but especially the crowd, hands on their heads or praying, had their eyes fixed on the ball. Time seemed to stand still, but everyone in Salt Lake City's Delta Center appeared to understand the story unfolding before them.

The moment, immortalized by NBA photographer Fernando Medina, was named the greatest photo in sports history by *Sports Illustrated* in 2012.

Beyond its artistic merit, this photo captures one of the most iconic moments of the NBA playoffs, and above all of Michael Jordan's career. It was precisely because this was supposed to be the last game of his career that it earned its place among the legendary moments of basketball history.

On June 14, 1998, the Bulls were leading the Utah Jazz 3–2 in the NBA Finals series. If they lost, MJ's team would be forced into a decisive Game 7. The Bulls were trailing by one point with 20 seconds left when Michael Jordan drove up the court, defended by Bryon Russell. The latter was about to feature, despite himself, on the poster. Unfortunately, he was on the wrong side of history.

His Airness attacked the basket with his right hand, performing a killer crossover by switching back to his left hand, while Bryon Russell faltered and even put his hand on the ground. Too late – Michael Jordan was all alone at the free-throw line. Number 23 rose up, the ball pierced the net as he held his arm outstretched towards the hoop, lingering in the pose. His team took the lead (87–86) with just 5.2 seconds remaining.

"I had no choice: it was do or die," he said after the game. "I let the clock run until I was in my favorite spot. As soon as Russell stuck to me, he made it easy for me. I drove, and he fell for the fake. I had a clear view of the basket."

A last-second shot by John Stockton missed the target, and the Bulls were NBA champions for the sixth time in their history, the third time in a row after 1996 and 1997. A sixth ring for the guard, who finished as MVP of the finals every time.

However, in the last minute of a breathless Game 6, Utah took a three-point lead with just over 40 seconds to go. That's when MJ decided to take matters into his own hands. He first reduced the gap by quickly scoring a layup (86–85). On the next play, he cleverly snatched the ball from Karl Malone's hands in the low post.

The rest is history, a scene worthy of a Hollywood film when His Majesty brought the ball back up to torment Bryon Russell for a 45th point that saved the game. "I think we've just witnessed Michael Jordan's best game-winning performance," said his coach, Phil Jackson. "He's proved it time and time again. Michael's the guy who's always there when it counts. He's a real-life hero."

Michael Jordan looks for a way out as he collides with Greg Foster.

MICHAEL JORDAN'S SIXTH AND FINAL TITLE

After his first three-peat in 1991, 1992, and 1993, Jordan retired for the first time to try his hand at baseball. Less than two years later, in March 1995, he was back in action with Chicago, on the way to completing another three-peat, capped off by "the Last Shot".

This shot was renamed as such because seven months later, in January 1999, Michael Jordan announced his retirement while the NBA was mired in a strike that paralyzed the league. He was "99.9 percent certain" that he would never play in the NBA again.

But in September 2001, Jordan returned to the court with the Washington Wizards, a team for which he was manager and co-owner. For the next two years, he played on the NBA courts in a new jersey, blue instead of red. He even shared a season with Bryon Russell, whom he continued to challenge in training. His decisive shot in Game 6 of the 1998 NBA Finals was therefore his last with his beloved team, the Chicago Bulls. A unique dynasty concluded in the most Jordan-esque way possible.

BULL
AZZ
34

8

2006

Kobe Bryant scores over 80!

On January 22, 2006, during a game that started badly for Los Angeles against the Raptors, "Black Mamba" suddenly woke up. Unleashed, surrounded by clumsy teammates, the Lakers guard exploded to break his personal record, with 81 points!

Lacking depth on the bench, the Toronto Raptors had been struggling since the start of the season, with just one win in 16 games. On the other side, now without Shaquille O'Neal, who had left for the Miami Heat, the Lakers were on the verge of total failure.

The only one to emerge was Kobe Bryant, who was keeping his head above water with 12 games of more than 40 points, including a record 62 points against the Dallas Mavericks. With two franchises in the doldrums, the crowd wasn't expecting any fireworks . . .

The day before, in true American fashion, Black Mamba overindulged in pizza and soda. To put it mildly, he had a slow, uneventful start. The Raptors, who were more energetic and effective from three-point range, took advantage in the first quarter.

Despite Toronto's comfortable lead (36–29), Kobe kept the Lakers afloat with 14 points and a few scattered but classy moves. Notably, there was a technical marvel of an up-and-under, not to mention a power layup executed against a stunned Jalen Rose. Then, thanks to surgical finishing and aggression in the face of sluggish teammates, the number 24 got the Lakers back on track.

A WAVE OF MADNESS

After starting the second quarter on the bench, Kobe Bryant forced some shots on his return but still managed to score 12 points. The team was finally getting into sync, and, with triangle plays serving the maestro, the Lakers' system looked more sophisticated. Black Mamba also made some impressive defensive moves, including a textbook screen on Chris Bosh, after a missed three-point attempt by Matt Bonner.

Just before the break, Bryant made his 62nd consecutive competitive free throw, before missing the 63rd. Unfazed by this setback, Kobe recovered on the rebound to score against a lackluster Raptors defense. Kobe reveled in a few clever in-and-outs to get around Toronto's "pillars," who were far too static against the absolute genius.

At the start of the second half, despite their guard's performance, the Lakers were trailing by 14 points (49–63). Kobe Bryant missed his first two shots at the start of the third quarter, which didn't bode well. Reassured by his devastating drives, he took advantage of the Raptors' generosity, led by Jalen Rose – who was too far away from him – to score basket after basket. Black Mamba's array of moves contributed to his most impressive game of the season.

However, despite his 47 points, the Raptors still led by 5. In the final stretch, just as the fans were beginning to realize that the game was going to go down in basketball history, Kobe Bryant reached the 61-point mark. Thanks to some wonderful off-the-dribble moves, the Lakers guard made the Raptors look like amateurs.

Los Angeles Lakers' Kobe Bryant (8) brings the ball up during the first quarter of their NBA game against the Toronto Raptors in Los Angeles on January 22, 2006. Bryant scored 81 points and set a personal single-game scoring high.

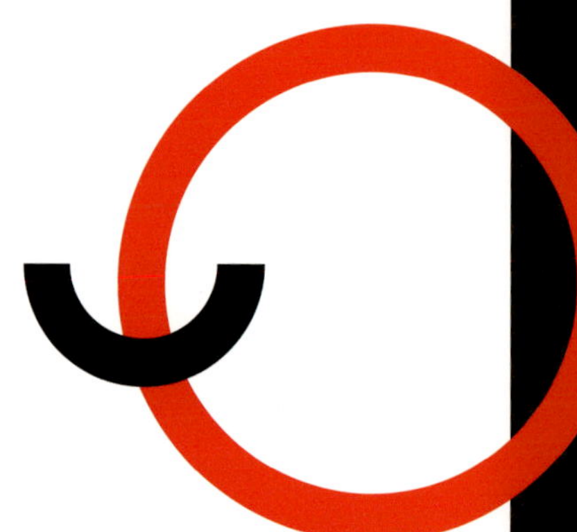

A MAGICAL MOMENT

Every pull-up sent the fans into a frenzy. Joey Graham tried to block KB, but the Mamba was now on a roll. There was only one person who could stop him in his tracks – his coach, Phil Jackson! Unfazed by the spectacular feats, Jackson wanted to give his leader a breather and call him back to the bench with five minutes to go. With flair, his assistant Brian Shawn stopped him. Kobe Bryant scored his last 7 points from free throws, reaching the incredible milestone of 81 points. Phil Jackson had the good sense to take his guard off the court with four seconds left, once the score was settled (122–104 to the Lakers). To the cheers of the crowd, Kobe Bryant raised his index finger to the sky like a Roman emperor who had just conquered hostile territory.

LAKERS
8

Cleveland Cavaliers forward LeBron James (23) has the ball knocked from his hands by San Antonio Spurs point guard Tony Parker (9) during first-half action in Game 4 of the NBA finals at Quicken Loans Arena on June 14, 2007, in Cleveland, Ohio.

2007

Tony Parker raises the French flag at the top of the NBA

At the end of a final perfectly controlled by the San Antonio Spurs against the Cleveland Cavaliers and a young LeBron James, French point guard Tony Parker became the first European MVP of the NBA Finals on June 14, 2007.

EUROPEANS TAKE OVER THE NBA

In recent years, regular season MVP titles have been shared by Europeans such as Greece's Giannis Antetokounmpo (2019 and 2020) and Serbia's Nikola Jokić (2021 and 2022). But at the beginning of the 21st century, such a flurry of talent from across the Atlantic didn't exist, and some players had to act as trailblazers for future generations.

June 14, 2007, marked a major breakthrough for European players in the NBA. With a French flag draped around his waist, Tony Parker was a happy man. He stood with his San Antonio teammates behind the Larry O'Brien Trophy, awarded to the NBA champion team. He had just won his third title a few minutes earlier against Cleveland.

In front of his friends, including 1998 World Cup champion footballer Thierry Henry, TP was called to the front of the stage and named MVP of the Finals. The first European to win the award, and the second non-American after Nigeria's Hakeem Olajuwon in 1994 and 1995.

"To have my name next to Michael Jordan's and Tim Duncan's in the MVPs is crazy. No one can ever take that away from me. It will be forever engraved on the MVP list," said the point guard after the game.

2007, THE YEAR OF TONY PARKER

As Tim Duncan's lieutenant for his first two big league titles, Tony Parker played a key role in 2007. He took the lead role alongside his teammates in the trio, which also included Argentine Manu Ginobili.

After successive wins over the Denver Nuggets, Phoenix Suns, and Utah Jazz, the Spurs faced the Cleveland Cavaliers in the final. The Ohio players were competing in their first NBA Finals, led by a young prodigy named LeBron James, a 22-year-old rookie at this level.

The entire basketball world predicted a bright future for LeBron, who went on to win four titles in nine finals. But in 2007, he was too isolated and showed a few weaknesses in his shooting, so his time had not yet come. At the age of 24, this was Tony Parker's year.

Right from the start of the series, the Normandy native made his mark at the AT&T Center in San Antonio. He was far too quick for the opposing defense, scoring 27 points in the first game and 30 in the second with devilish accuracy (65 percent success rate). Before moving to the Quicken Loans Arena in Cleveland, the Spurs were already leading two games to none.

In Game 3, TP was less successful. Despite only scoring 17 points, he still finished as his team's top scorer and, more importantly, helped his team win with a decisive shot in the final minute. His team took a 5-point lead and never looked back, earning themselves a chance to clinch the series. Two days later, San Antonio had the opportunity to end the season by sweeping their opponents, leaving them without a single win in the series. Once again, Tony Parker stepped up to lead the Texans to victory thanks to his 24 points, ably assisted by Manu Ginobili (27 points). The Argentinian put an end to the suspense by scoring two final free throws with less than two seconds remaining. Overall, TP dominated the final, proving unstoppable for the Cavs' defense with 24.5 points on 57 percent shooting, 5 rebounds, and 3 assists per game in the series. Unsurprisingly, the Frenchman was named the best player of the finals, entering the pantheon of basketball legends and, more broadly, French sports legends.

That same year, Dirk Nowitzki (of the Dallas Mavericks) became the first European MVP of the regular season. Tony Parker symbolized the NBA's increasing openness to equally talented basketball players from across the Atlantic and, more broadly, from around the world. However, Nowitzki (2011) and Giannis Antetokounmpo (2021) remain the only Europeans to have succeeded Tony Parker as Finals MVP.

Daniel Gibson of the Cleveland Cavaliers takes the ball from Tony Parker.

PARKER
9

Tony Parker (9) leads the French team to victory in the European Basketball Championship with Lithuania's Mantas Kalnietis (5) behind him.

2013

The coronation of an entire blue generation

On September 22, 2013, the French men's team won the first title in its history by beating Lithuania (80–66) in the EuroBasket final, rewarding the many sacrifices made by the Parker generation.

It was 10.36 pm when the buzzer sounded in the Stožice Arena in Ljubljana, Slovenia. Nicolas Batum, Nando de Colo, Alexis Ajinça, Joffrey Lauvergne, and Thomas Heurtel congratulated each other, gathered in a circle. Off to the side, Florent Piétrus made his way over to Tony Parker. The embrace between the two men is as sincere as it is moving, the former whispering a few words into the latter's ear while cupping his head in his hands.

We'll never really know what the two teammates said to each other, but that image is worth a thousand words. It represents a generation finally rewarded with an international title after years of sacrifice – and failures – every summer.

A WELL-DESERVED VICTORY

Due to a strong start from Lithuanian power forward Linas Kleiza (20 points in total, including 16 in the first half), Les Bleus were struggling at the end of the first quarter (19–22). It was in the second half that the French team took the lead, with Nicolas Batum in top form – scoring all 17 of his points in the first half – with plenty of help from the bench. Johan Petro, Nando de Colo, Florent Piétrus, and Antoine Diot made up for Tony Parker's clumsiness (4 points at 2/7 at the break). Diot's killer shot from the middle of the court as the half-time siren sounded gave the French a 16-point lead (50–34).

Les Bleus posed a multifaceted offensive threat. After the break, it was Boris Diaw who racked up the points near the basket. By scoring 13 of his 15 points after half-time, he helped extend France's lead even further (60–41).

Despite a change in defense and the revival of Mantas Kalnietis (19 points), Lithuania failed to catch up with the French. On the other side, Tony Parker finally found his stride, scoring 8 points in the final minutes. The score was too wide, and the clock

was ticking down as France celebrated their European title (80–66). In hindsight, the final seemed too easy for Les Bleus, as if they had already won the title two days earlier in the semifinals against Spain (75–72 after overtime). Of the 2013 European campaign, French fans remember this summit meeting more than anything else.

THE TERRIBLE FRANCO-SPANISH RIVALRY

At every international competition, the two teams seem destined to meet as soon as the final phase begins. The thing is, France often loses the Spanish. The French team had already stumbled against La Roja in the quarterfinals of Euro 2009 (86–66), and, more importantly, in the final of Euro 2011 (98-85), and then went on to lose in the quarterfinals of the 2012 London Olympics (66–50).

The wound was deep and, in 2013, history seemed to be repeating itself. Spain extended its lead in the second quarter thanks to Les Bleus' clumsy three-point shooting (0/8 at the break). Only Tony Parker was keeping his head above water, scoring 14 of his team's 20 points at half-time, while Boris Diaw tried to spark a comeback with a violent foul on Sergio Llull (34–20). It was in the locker room that the game turned around. In front of his teammates, head down, Tony Parker delivered a memorable rant, which still resonates today thanks to the Canal+ cameras that captured the moment.

"They're dominating us because they think we're s***, and you can see it on their faces. I don't care what happens in the second half, even if we lose, at least we'll play with pride," he told his teammates.

In the second half, they came back with renewed energy. Antoine Diot scored two long-range shots and Florent Piétrus gave Marc Gasol a hard time, while Tony Parker

continued to terrify the opposition with his skill (32 points in total). Flawless from the free throw line (8/9), Parker pushed Spain into overtime. During this period, Antoine Diot sealed the victory from the free throw line. The final score was 75–72, a victory that already felt like a title.

"It's the greatest victory in the history of French basketball," said Tony Parker after the game. Just two days later, in the final, a new chapter was written as they claimed the European title against Lithuania. Unsurprisingly, TP was named MVP of the competition.

The French team celebrates its victory over Lithuania during the European basketball championship final in Ljubljana, September 22, 2013.

Evan Fournier (left) and Jrue Holiday (right) go head-to-head.

2021

France, Team USA's new nemesis

There's no better way to kick off the Olympic Games. From the start of the Tokyo Olympics, facing the United States, the overwhelming favorites and three-time defending Olympic champions, Les Bleus achieved a major feat on July 25, 2021.

The French team managed to topple the American giants (83–76), who had won 25 consecutive Olympic Games since their semifinal defeat by Argentina in 2004 (89–81). Even better, after their first victory two years earlier in the quarterfinals of the 2019 World Cup (89–79), the French team became the first team to beat Team USA twice in a row in the World Cup and Olympic finals since 1992 and the arrival of NBA players in the national team.

THE UNDERDOGS

France's coach Vincent Collet once again got the better of his counterpart, Spurs legend and five-time NBA champion Gregg Popovich. With three losses in as many warm-up games, the French team was not in the best shape going into the match against the competition favorites, who were chasing their 16th Olympic crown.

The United States started the game on the front foot, taking an 8-point lead at the break (45–37). Despite nine turnovers and poor shooting (1/11 from three-point range), France was not far behind and could still hope for a comeback in the second half. This was especially true as the game turned in the early stages of the third quarter when American star Kevin Durant picked up his fourth foul (24th minute). With him off the court to avoid a fifth and disqualifying foul, France took advantage to step up a gear. Trailing 49–40 at the start of the second half, they turned the game around to finish the third quarter with a six-point lead (62–56).

TEAM USA NEVER DIED

With four minutes remaining, the Americans regained a seven-point lead (74–67). But then their offensive machine stalled, faltered, and couldn't find the basket for more than three minutes, making mistake after mistake.

France, meanwhile, chipped away at the deficit before Evan Fournier delivered the final blow. Scoring a total of 28 points, the French guard put his team back in front with one minute to go with a long-range shot (76–74). Guerschon Yabusele's selflessness in saving the ball from going out of bounds and slipping it to Evan Fournier symbolized the French team's determination.

In the end, Les Bleus held their nerve from the free throw line to secure a prestigious victory. However, there was no time for celebrations for the French team, as they still had a long way to go to achieve their goal of reaching the final against the USA. "We won against the best team in the tournament, but we mustn't get carried away," said captain Nicolas Batum. "We need to stay focused on the game against the Czech Republic in three days' time. We want to go far, but we have to remain humble."

After two more controlled group matches against the Czech Republic (97–77) and Iran (79–62), France eliminated Italy in the quarterfinals (84–75) and then Slovenia in the semifinals thanks to a decisive block by Nicolas Batum with two seconds left on the clock (90–89).

In the final on August 7, France again faced the United States, who were

obviously out for revenge against their new nemesis. Much more enterprising than in the opening game, and above all less troubled by fouls, Kevin Durant dominated this final with 29 total points.

France's dreams began to take shape again when Frank Ntilikina slammed home a primed basket with just over five minutes to go, bringing the score to within three points. But this time, Team USA held on, beating Les Bleus (87–82) for the third time in Olympic final history, after 1948 and 2000.

Evan Fournier's teammates might harbor some regrets after his less accurate performance. By losing 19 balls (compared to six for the USA), they gave their opponents too much ammunition. "We could have won this game," Fournier said afterwards.

Rudy Gobert and the entire French team got off to a flying start.

Guerschon Yabusele of France goes in for a score against Team USA's Stephen Curry (4) and LeBron James (6) in a game where Team USA beat France 98–87 for the gold medal in the Paris 2024 Olympics

2024

Stephen Curry takes over Bercy and kills France's dream

Just when the French team was dreaming of revenge for Tokyo 2021 and a first Olympic gold medal, Stephen Curry shattered an entire country's dream with a titanic performance and an exceptional game.

There are some moves, some moments of transcendence that mark finals or tournaments more than others. Sometimes, a crunch time alone is enough to make a match legendary. At the Bercy Arena, in the final of the Paris 2024 Olympic basketball tournament against host nation France, Stephen Curry did all that. Well established in the hierarchy of the best players in NBA history, the Warriors point guard had never made his mark on the international stage with Team USA, despite two successful world campaigns in 2010 and 2014. So for his first Olympics, the two-time MVP had to go big, and France paid the price.

After a disappointing group stage, Les Bleus were not looking forward to the rest of their tournament. Swept aside by Germany, they gave themselves a scare against Brazil and Japan and found themselves facing the Canadians in the quarterfinals. However, boosted by an internal shock and a major row with federation president Jean-Pierre Siutat, Les Bleus refocused and beat Canada and then Germany, the reigning world champions. On fire in both games, Isaïa Cordinier even allowed himself the luxury of a remarkable statement: "I'm sorry, but the truth is, we're thugs! And when we play like thugs, this is what happens!" Les Bleus were in the final, and it was nothing short of a miracle.

CURRY MADNESS

Meanwhile, the Americans cruised through the group stage and quarterfinals against Brazil (122–87). But in the semifinals, they had a real scare against a conquering Serbian team. Trailing by 13 points at the start of the final quarter, in a game where they were down by as many as 17 points, they rallied to win, led by Lebron James, Kevin Durant, and Stephen Curry. The latter, who had been quiet in the group stage (averaging 7.3 points), stepped up his game in the final stages, averaging 22.3 points per game. This was mainly thanks to his stunning semifinal performance against Serbia, where he scored 36 points and made nine three-pointers. He wouldn't falter in the final either.

In a packed Bercy Arena, not entirely won over to the French cause, Curry ended France's dreams. Les Bleus looked a little off their game and trailed by around 10 points for much of the match, but they rallied at the end to close the gap to just three points with three minutes to go. Anything was possible. On a night when Isaïa Cordinier (0 points) and Evan Fournier (8) couldn't get going, Guerschon Yabusele (20) and Victor Wembanyama (26) stepped up. Almost single-handedly, and with welcome support from Nando De Colo, the two big men gave Les Bleus something to dream about.

Except that Stephen Curry was determined not to let anyone take away his first Olympic title, so he pulled out all the stops. In 2 minutes and 12 seconds, the point guard sunk four three-pointers in four attempts, each one crazier and more complicated than the last, ending the dreams of the stunned French team, which finished 11 points behind (87–98). With his famous "night, night" gesture, Curry sealed the deal, leaving Les Bleus out cold.

YABUSELE POSTERIZES LEBRON

While France lost big on August 10, 2024, Guerschon Yabusele can console himself with the most defining play of the Games on the court, one that will stand out across all competitions, right to the end – a huge dunk on LeBron James. After a move to the basket, Yabusele rose up to the rim and slammed home a devastating dunk over one of the best players in history! In disbelief, LeBron called for a foul, which never came. With his butt on the floor, LeBron had just been posterized by Yabusele, who would return to the 76ers the following summer.

While this final owed much of its epic nature to Stephen Curry's talent, it also owed a lot to Victor Wembanyama in his first major appearance against Team USA. Predicted to dominate the NBA in the coming years, the young Frenchman showed why the United States should be concerned that their international dominance might not last. At just 20 years old and with 26 points and 7 rebounds, the rising star of French basketball was impressive in his first major international competition and has set his sights on Los Angeles 2028. And this time, LeBron James, Stephen Curry, and Kevin Durant won't be there . . .

Stephen Curry (6) during the final gold medal game between Team USA and Team France at the Paris 2024 Summer Olympic Games on August 10, 2024.

PHOTO CREDITS

p.ii and cover: Alamy; pp.iv–v: ©Nuccio DiNuzzo/Chicago Tribune/TNS/ABACAPRESS.COM By Icon Sport/ Abaca/ Icon Sport; p.viii: © MANTEY STEPHANE/ PRESSE SPORTS; p.2: © DESCHAMPS MICHEL/ PRESSES SPORTS; p.4: © chippix/ Shutterstock; p.7: © oneinchpunch/ Shutterstock; p.8: ©Malcolm Emmons-USA TODAY Network/ IconSport; p.9: ©Ed Wagner Jr./Chicago Tribune/TNS/Sipa USA/ Icon Sport; p.10: ©Newspix / Icon Sport; p.11 above: © Winslow Townson-USA TODAY Sports/Sipa USA/ Icon sport; p.11 below: ©Kirby Lee-USA TODAY Sports/Sipa USA/ Icon Sport; p.12 (inset) : ©Malcolm Emmons-USA TODAY Sports/USA Today Network/Sipa USA/ Icon Sport; p12: ©Manny Rubio-USA TODAY Sports/ SUSA / Icon Sport; pp.14, 15: ©Malcolm Emmons-USA TODAY Sports/USA Today Network/Sipa USA/ Icon Sport; p.16 (inset) Alamy; p.16: ©Kamil Krzaczynski-USA TODAY Sports/Sipa USA/ Icon Sport: pp.18–19: ©Jeff Hanisch-USA TODAY Sports/Sipa USA/ Icon Sport; p.20 (inset): ©Firo/ Icon Sport; p.20: ©Bill Streicher/USA TODAY SPORTS/PRESSE SPORTS; p.22: ©Photoshot / Icon Sport; p.23: ©Jaime Valdez/ USA TODAY Sports/ PRESSE SPORTS; p.24 (inset): ©Rob Schumacher/The Arizona Republic via USA TODAY NETWORK/ Icon Sport; ©PictureAlliance / Icon Sport; p.26: ©Photo by US PRESSWIRE/USA Today Network/Sipa USA/ Icon Sport; p.27: ©New York Knicks Photo/ Icon Sport; p.28 (inset): Wikicommons; p.28: Alamy; p.31 (inset): Alamy; p.31: ©Photo by Darryl Norenberg-USA TODAY Sports Network/USA Today Network/Sipa USA/ Icon Sport; p.34: ©Icon Sport; p.32: ©MPS/USA TODAY SPORTS/PRESSE SPORTS; p.35: ©LUTTIAU/ PRESSE SPORTS; p.36: ©Newspix / Icon Sport; p.38: ©USA TODAY SPORTS/PRESSE SPORTS; p.39: ©Newspix / Icon Sport; p.40 (inset): Alamy; p.40: ©Chris Humphreys/USA TODAY SPORTS/PRESSE SPORTS; p.42: ©Jim Rassol-USA TODAY Sports/Sipa USA/ Icon Sport; p.43: ©Bill Streicher-USA TODAY Sports NBA: Playoffs-Miami Heat at Philadelphia 76ers/PRESSE SPORTS; p.44 (inset): ©Icon Sport; p.44: ©Darryl Norenberg-US PRESSWIRE/USA Today Network/ Sipa USA/ Icon Sport; p.47: ©Malcolm Emmons-USA TODAY Sports/USA Today Network/Sipa USA/ Icon Sport; p.48 (inset): ©Darren Yamashita-USA TODAY Sports/ Sipa USA/ Icon Sport; p.48: ©Paul Rutherford-USA TODAY Sports/PRESSE SPORTS; p.50: ©Kyle Terada-USA TODAY Sports/Sipa USA/ Icon Sport; p.51: ©K. Terada/US PRESSWIRE/PRESSE SPORTS; pp.52, 54: Alamy; p.56: Javier Mendia García/Wikicommons; p.57: ©Tommy Gilligan-USA TODAY Sports/Sipa USA/ Icon Sport; p.58: © Geoff Burke/USA TODAY Sports/Sipa USA/ Icon Sport; p.59: © Liga ACB Photo/ Shot For Press / Icon Sport; pp.60, 62, 63: Alamy; p.64 (inset): ©Brad Penner-USA TODAY Sports / PRESSE SPORTS; p.64: ©Kamil Krzaczynski-USA TODAY Sports / PRESSE SPORTS; p.67: ©M.Emmons/US PRESSWIRE/PRESSE SPORTS; p.68 (inset): ©Vincent Carchietta-USA TODAY Sports/ Sipa USA/ Icon Sport; pp.68, 71: © Bill Streicher-USA TODAY Sports/Sipa USA/ Icon Sport; pp.72, 75: Alamy; p.76 (inset): ©Marca / Icon Sport; p.76: © NBA Photo/ Cal Sport Media / Icon Sport; p.79: ©Amandine Noel / Icon Sport; p.80 (inset): ©Russ Isabella- USA TODAY Sports/Sipa USA/ Icon Sport; p.80: ©Jean Paul Thomas / Icon Sport; p.82: ©PA Images / Icon Sport; p.83: ©Jeffrey Swinger-USA TODAY Sports/Sipa USA/ Icon Sport; pp.84, 87: Alamy; p.88 (inset): ©Photoshot / Icon Sport; p.88: ©Kyle Terada-USA TODAY Sports/Sipa USA/ Icon Sport; p.90: ©Thomas Shea-USA TODAY Sports/ Sipa USA/ Icon Sport; p.91: ©Dave Winter / Icon Sport; p.92 (inset): ©Icon Sport; p.92: ©PictureAlliance / Icon Sport; p.94: ©UPI / Icon Sport; p.95: ©Phil O'Brien / PA Images / Icon Sport; p.96 (inset): ©Photoshot / Icon Sport; p.96: ©Patrick D. Witty/Chicago Tribune/TNS/ABACAPRESS.COM By Icon Sport/ Abaca/ Icon Sport; p.98: ©Anne Ryan-USA TODAY Photo by Icon Sport/ SUSA/ Icon Sport; p.99 (left): ©PictureAlliance / Icon Sport; p.99 (right): ©WireImage / Icon Sport; p.100 (inset): © NUCCIO DINUZZO/ SUSA / Icon Sport; p.100: ©PHIL VELASQUEZ/ Photo by TB/ SUSA / Icon Sport; p.103: ©Photo by Mary Jo Walicki/Milwaukee Journal Sentinel/KRT/ SUSA/ Icon Sport; p.104 (inset): Alamy; p.104: John Zich / AP Photo; p.107: Alamy; p.108: ©DESCHAMPS MICHEL/ PRESSE SPORTS; p.108 (inset): ©DESCHAMPS MICHEL/ PRESSE SPORTS; p.110: ©CATHERINE STEENKESTE/ PRESSE SPORTS; p.111: ©PictureAlliance / Icon Sport; pp.112, 114, 115: Alamy; p.116 (inset): ©Upi / Icon Sport; p.116: ©Photoshot / Icon Sport; p.119: ©Upi / Icon Sport; p.120 (inset): Edgars2007 / Wikicommons; p.120: ©Chamid / Icon Sport; p.122: ©Michael Ponomarenko / Icon Sport; p 123: ©Primoz Lavre / Icon Sport; p.124 (inset): ©Michael Steele / PA Images / Icon Sport; p.124: ©DESCHAMPS MICHEL/ PRESSE SPORTS; p.126–127: ©Icon Sport; ©PictureAlliance / Icon Sport; pp.128–131: Alamy; p.132 (inset): ©Icon Sport; p.132: ©DESCHAMPS MICHEL/ PRESSE SPORTS; p.134: ©Photo by US PRESSWIRE/ USA Today Network/Sipa USA/ Icon Sport; p.135: ©Photo by US PRESSWIRE/USA Today Network/Sipa USA/ Icon Sport; p.139: ©Malcolm Emmons/USA TODAY SPORTS/PRESSE SPORTS; p.136 (inset) / ©Gerry Cranham/OFFSIDE/ PRESSE SPORTS; p.136: Gerry Cranham/ OFFSIDE/PRESSE SPORTS; p.140 (inset): ©Photo by OR/ SUSA/ Icon Sport; p.140: ©Photoshot / Icon Sport; p.143: ©Photoshot / Icon Sport; pp.144–147: Alamy; p.148 (inset): ©Kyle Terada-USA TODAY Sports/Sipa USA/ Icon Sport; p.148: © Jed Jacobsohn/ USA TODAY Sports/Sipa USA/ Icon Sport; p.151: © Kyle Terada-USA TODAY Sports/Sipa USA/ Icon Sport; p.152 (inset): ©Mark J. Rebilas-USA TODAY Sports/Sipa USA / Icon Sport; p.152 / ©Brendan Maloney/US PRESSWIRE/PRESSE SPORTS; p.155: ©Brad Mills-USA TODAY Sports/Sipa USA/ Icon Sport; p.156: ©Photo by Malcolm Emmons-USA TODAY Sports/USA Today Network/Sipa USA/ Icon Sport; p.159: Alamy; p.160: Alamy; p.162–163: ©PictureAlliance/ Icon Sport; p.164: Alamy; p.167: ©Icon Sport; p.168: ©Photo by TB/ SUSA/ Icon Sport; p.171: Alamy; p.172: ©Robert Hanashiro-USA TODAY Photo/ SUSA/ Icon Sport; p.175: ©Anne Ryan-USA TODAY/ SUSA/ Icon Sport; p.176, 179, 180: Alamy; p.183: ©Ed Suba Jr./Akron Beacon Journal/TNS/ ABACAPRESS.COM/ Icon Sport; p.184: Alamy; pp.186–187: ©Primoz Lavre / Icon Sport; pp.188, 190: ©Photo by Anthony Dibon/Icon; pp.192, 195: Alamy. Jerseys: shutterstock.com and Designed by Freepik, www.freepik.com